September 16, 2011

Tiffany –

Rule #1 : Never ~~punt on~~ First down.

Rule # 2 : We'll always be your Cheerleaders

We hope this book inspires you & Brian to create your own personal football team! Go Team Demos!
Love ya –
Kathy & Ginger

spouses to strive for a higher level of energy, perseverance, and ultimate satisfaction in their relationship."

—JERAMY and JERUSHA CLARK, authors of *Define the Relationship* and *I Gave Dating a Chance*

"*Extreme Marriage* is what every married or unmarried couple should read. It helps you understand daily struggles and opens your eyes to what is most important in a relationship."

—SETH KIMBROUGH, professional BMX rider and singer with Mortal Treason

super bowl marriage

from training camp

to the championship game

TERRY OWENS

FOREWORD BY MIKE SINGLETARY

WATERBROOK
PRESS

SUPER BOWL MARRIAGE
PUBLISHED BY WATERBROOK PRESS
12265 Oracle Blvd., Suite 200
Colorado Springs, Colorado 80921
A division of Random House, Inc.

All Scripture quotations, unless otherwise indicated, are taken from the *Holy Bible, New International Version*®. NIV®. Copyright © 1973, 1978, 1984 by International Bible Society. Used by permission of Zondervan Publishing House. All rights reserved. Scripture quotations marked (MSG) are taken from *The Message.* Copyright © 1993, 1994, 1995, 1996, 2000, 2001, 2002. Used by permission of NavPress Publishing Group.

ISBN 1-57856-882-X

Library of Congress Cataloging-in-Publication Data
Owens, Terry, 1956–
  Super Bowl marriage : from training camp to the championship game / Terry Owens.—1st ed.
        p. cm.
  Includes bibliographical references.
  ISBN 1-57856-882-X
  1. Husbands—Religious life.   2. Marriage—Religious aspects—Christianity.
3. Super Bowl—Miscellanea.   I. Title.
  BV4528.3.O94 2005
  248.8'425—dc22

                        2005016220

Printed in the United States of America
2005—First Edition

10 9 8 7 6 5 4 3 2 1

contents

Foreword

"We interrupt this marriage to bring you…football season."

Several years ago my wife, Kim, found a pillow with that inscription on it at a craft show. She brought it home and showed it to me. I can honestly say I didn't even give it a thought. But if I had, my thoughts would have been something like this: *Yeah, we're interrupting this marriage for football season.* Football *is what gives us this home you're living in.* Football *is what affords us that nice car you're driving. I have set goals for my career. I'm trying to be the best linebacker I can be, the best defensive player ever. And, in order to do that, I need to devote my all to football.*

As for that pillow, the sad reality is that football "season" was year-round. Right after the last Bears' game, my mind started preparing for next season. I took a month or so off for my body to rest, but in my mind I began setting goals for off-season training.

With every new season, I had a list of new goals. The only goals that weren't met were occasional team goals, like going to the playoffs or the Super Bowl. My personal goals? I met every one. Because I'm a goal setter by nature, I made goals for everything—even my family. But those goals were vague: "Be the best family we can be" and "Have our kids respect us." By contrast, my personal training goals were very specific, with a plan of action for each. In my mind, the fact that I even *had* family goals put me way above most guys I knew, even though I didn't attack those goals with any intensity.

I was blessed to retire at my own will. I remained healthy through-out my career and chose to call it quits after twelve years with the Bears. Most guys are not that fortunate; an injury or two forces the retirement. At that time we had three children under six, and Kim was expecting our fourth any day. I learned rather quickly that there was a system—a routine she had developed over the years—and her expectations were for me to fall in line. My expectations were to rock the boat.

We were warned about how difficult retirement would be. I had prepared financially for this time. What I didn't prepare for was Kim's reaction to my retirement. In essence, she thought that since there would be no more interruptions in the marriage for football, it was time to focus on her and the kids. And the real tragedy was that I thought I *had* been focused on them! How much more could she need?

Since we'd met at Baylor University, where I was playing foot-ball, she'd never known me outside of football. Through the years it was easy for her to see how detailed I was in my preparation and focus for the football season. And she knew that she never received even a portion of my preparation and focus for herself.

I've now spent ten years out of football, and in those ten years God has finally driven the message home to me that our marriage and our seven children require *more* than the effort I put into the game of football. Our children's lives are at stake. Their spiritual des-tinies are at stake. Our marriage is the foundation of it all.

During those ten years since the end of my football career, I have often traveled around the country for motivational speaking engagements. Approximately once a week I have found myself on an airplane, usually in first class, with a corporate executive next to me. Many of them, both male and female, had made it to the top, achieved incredible success, and reached all of their goals. But I found a disturbing trend in the number who had done it at the expense of their families. Many were on second and third marriages and had estranged relationships with their children. And most were lonely and unfulfilled.

In my heart I always believed that family was the most important thing in my life. I knew it was. What I didn't know was that I needed to be proactive in my approach. The 1985 Chicago Bears had a very specific plan of attack for getting to the Super Bowl that year. Not difficult. Just determined. We went on to become one of the most memorable teams in Super Bowl history.

My pride is stripped. My priorities have shifted. I now have a new list of goals. For the first time in my life, God has given me success at home *and* success in my career. My prayer is that you will experience a Super Bowl marriage too. There is nothing like it!

—Mike Singletary

To Tari,
a teammate in life who has helped me become
a much better player,
and
my mother and late father,
whose love and stable home gave me the freedom
to play and learn

Acknowledgments

I sometimes sit in my office at home, staring in disbelief at a book cover with my name on it. Though my name appears on the cover, this is not my book. I'm only one player on a great team. Without my teammates, on this project and in life, there would be no book. By acknowledging them, I'm also acknowledging the wisdom of God, His design of community, and the role we play in each other's lives.

I'm grateful to the people at WaterBrook Press. The relationship between a writer and his editors exerts a powerful influence on a book. I have had the privilege to work with two excellent editors. Bruce helped shape my thoughts and words, especially early in the process. His wise oversight and insightful observations made the writing much stronger. Carol brought a fresh perspective to later drafts. When I thought we were pretty much done, her thoughtful questions challenged me to keep going. Ginia, Joel, Stephanie, and Jessica are other members of the WaterBrook team. I can't imagine a project like this without the creativity and commitment of people like them.

I also can't imagine a project like this without the insights, belief, and encouragement of Tari, my own marriage teammate. We're a great team, but there are others on my marriage team, men whose friendship and commitment to their own marriages have made me a better husband. I'm grateful for what "brothers" like Finny, Joe, Taylor, and Jon add to my life.

There are men ahead of me whose lives and marriages remind me that my biggest challenges, and most satisfying victories, may be yet to come. The examples of Mike, Rick, and George encourage me to stay strong.

Finally, I'm deeply grateful to the people I interviewed for the different chapters. Their willingness to share humbles me, and their stories inspire me. If I've done my job on the team, they'll inspire you as well.

Introduction

marriage is simpler than we make it. *Oh really?* Follow me on this.

I grew up loving sports—baseball, basketball, and football. I played them. I watched them. And I learned from them, all of them. But I connected with football on a deeper level than the others.

Maybe it was the contact, the man-on-man physicalness of blocking and tackling, that made the competition more direct, more personal. Maybe the diversity of the positions and the size and skills of the athletes who played them made the concept of team more apparent. Perhaps ten-play drives and fourteen-game seasons helped me understand how important each moment and each day are to reaching a bigger goal. Whatever the reasons, football taught me lessons that no other sport did.

If you have ever played the game at any level or even watched a lot of football, you learned lessons as well—relationship skills, for instance. Think about it: A football team is a group of individuals in relationship with each other, connected by their devotion to a single goal. The better the players, the more passionate their commitment, the clearer their focus, and the more connected they are as a team, the greater their success. In a similar way, the characteristics that make great players and great teams also make great husbands and great marriages.

This book will show you how to transfer what you have learned about relationships and teamwork in football to your marriage. And we're going to have fun in the process. Each chapter begins with a story about an NFL team, player, or game. Rather than identify the subject of the chapter up-front, the stories are told by a succession of clues. It's NFL trivia, and the challenge for you is to identify the team, player, or game before you get through the first half of the chapter. At that point I "solve" the mystery, in case you haven't, and we transition into the marriage application.

For example, what better way to learn how successful teams are built than to examine one of the most successful teams of all time? Chapter 2 begins with the fourth player taken in the 1969 draft— the first player drafted by the new coach of an abysmal team. Three years later, after the 1972 season, they won their first playoff game in twenty-five years when the most controversial play in the history of the NFL went their way. But it was their 1974 draft, the league's best ever, that launched them into a run of Super Bowl dominance that has never been equaled. By reflecting on how that team was built, we can see how to build an increasingly effective marriage team.

Each chapter concludes with The Extra Point where you're put into a football scenario. I encourage you to read them and to imagine it really is you in the situation. How would you respond? And how do you respond to similar situations in marriage? Getting the extra point will help you apply the chapter to yourself and your marriage. A small thing, but it could be the difference between winning and losing, between going deep into the playoffs and, to paraphrase Joe Montana, sitting at home with everyone else, watching the Super Bowl.

Revolutionary approaches, incredible comebacks, awe-inspiring efforts, last-minute drives, comical resourcefulness—see what happens when players never lose sight of their championship goal. And imagine what could happen if we brought that same spirit to our marriages. I think you'll find that marriage is simpler than we think it is, if we learn to think about it differently than we usually do. If we think about it like a football game.

Are you up for the challenge of this book? Are you up for the challenge of a Super Bowl marriage?

A Little Different Approach

*One thing I learned working as an assistant
coach under Bill Walsh with the 49ers
is you don't build championship teams
with a blueprint for a 9-7 team.*

—Dennis Green

[I t] still amounts to nothing more than a total attention to detail and an appreciation for every facet of offensive football and refinement of those things that are needed to provide an environment that allows people to perform at their maximum levels of self-actualization," the coach said of his revolutionary new offense.

Hmmmm. What ever happened to "three yards and a cloud of dust"?

It's quite likely that this guy never saw offensive football as three yards and a cloud of dust. He's not what you'd call a simplistic thinker. He has a master's degree in education and has always loved to teach. Though originally a defensive coach, it was opposing offensive coaches who proved most influential in his early development.

And none more so than Sid Gillman, father of the modern passing game. As a coach with the Oakland Raiders in 1966, this man got the chance to study Gillman's San Diego Chargers.

However, the legendary Paul Brown was to be the strongest influence of all. This man worked as an offensive coach under Brown from 1968 to 1975. It was Brown's second tour of duty in the league, this time with the expansion Cincinnati Bengals. Brown's willingness to let his coaches coach created the perfect laboratory. And he also allowed his assistants total autonomy in building the team.

The Bengals' need for innovation was evident from day one. Their offensive line was not overpowering. Neither was their quarterback's arm or the defense, for that matter. It was an ideal scenario for a creative young coach eager to earn his props. He thought the team could stay competitive against superior opponents if they could control the ball by using short, precisely timed passes to generate twenty-five first downs a game. The Bengals' willingness to throw on any down and from anywhere on the field loudly defied the prevailing offensive strategies.

The ideas the coach had begun experimenting with in 1968 as a way to help his undermanned team stay competitive had become an effective offensive system. And in 1979 the coach was named head coach and general manager of another overmatched team, a 2-14 doormat. The team's second straight 2-14 record in his first year had to be discouraging. But he followed that with a hopeful 6-8 second season. They improved to an NFL-best 13-3 the following year and earned a trip to the NFC championship game.

Their opponent was familiar. The two teams had taken turns embarrassing each other during their last two meetings, but the coach had to like his chances on his home field. Only one problem: the visitors were the NFC's elite. They'd been to five of the first fifteen Super Bowls and had won it twice. They were talented, confident, and experienced.

The home team scored first, quieting any doubts about whether they belonged in the championship game. The visitors then answered with a field goal and a touchdown. This was the first of six lead changes in the game. The teams traded touchdowns in the second quarter. The upstarts regained the lead with a touchdown in the third quarter, that period's only score. The proper order of the NFL was restored in the fourth, as the playoff-savvy visitors scored a field goal and a touchdown to go up 27–21. That's where things stood when the home team took over at their own 11 with 4:54 left.

Doubts about whether or not the coach and his young team belonged on the same field with their storied opponents had been answered. Doubts about whether or not his offense could stand up to playoff pressure persisted. The home team had lost three fumbles, and the quarterback had thrown three interceptions.

Time for a little offensive genius. The coach knew the defense would be playing prevent, so he called runs on three of the first five plays. The strategy worked as they advanced the ball to their own 41. A penalty and a 5-yard completion moved the ball into their opponent's territory at the two-minute warning. Another run and two completed passes moved the ball to a first down at the 13. Time-out with 1:15 left.

"Water, gimme some water," gasped one of the wideouts to a trainer. The receiver, a former tenth-round draft pick, had collapsed due to exhaustion and the effects of the flu he'd battled all week. He may have been sick, and tired, but he wasn't coming out. Not now. Not with history about to be written.

"[He] had that uncanny knack of being able to find a hole in the defense" is how the quarterback, taken in the third round of the same draft, remembered the wideout. "When you were in trouble, he was always trying to come back to help you. He never stopped working."

After an incompletion, a 7-yard run pushed the ball to the 6, where they called another time-out. Fifty-eight seconds remained. The coach and the quarterback huddled on the sideline, planning the next two plays. Brown Left Slot-Sprint Right Option was the first. It was a staple of their goal-line offense, a play they had practiced hundreds of times. They had also scored on it earlier in the game.

"Look for Freddie," the coach reminded the quarterback. "Hold it…or throw it high for [the secondary receiver] so that if he can't get it, it'll be thrown away." The dehydrated wideout was the second choice on the play. He was to screen the defender off the primary receiver, then slide across the back of the end zone, just in case.

The play started badly. Freddie slipped and couldn't shake his man. The rush broke through and chased the quarterback out of the pocket. He headed for the sideline, buying time and hoping some-body would get open. He knew he couldn't take the sack. Winner take all on fourth-and-long was not what they wanted. But he was nearly out of bounds with two defenders only a couple of yards away. He had to do something—and fast.

The quarterback couldn't see the secondary receiver, much less if he was open. But after practicing this play so many times, he knew where he'd be. The QB turned his body toward the goalposts, stepped away from the rush, threw off his back foot, and got ham-mered to the ground. The pass flew high, just the way they'd talked about it. Touchdown or fourth down? One man would determine which.

The hard-working, flu-stricken, six-foot-four receiver jumped as high and reached as far as he could. He clawed the ball with his fingertips and juggled it briefly. His left foot landed just inside the back line, then his right, as he pulled the ball to his chest. He took two steps before celebrating with the most understated spike in the history of big-time catches.

"The play has always been called The Catch, and that's just what it was. The Catch," insisted the quarterback, giving credit where credit was due. "It wasn't a bad pass—I wasn't throwing it away; Dwight said it was a perfect pass, any lower and Walls would have batted it away—but it sure wasn't The Pass."

Walls—the Dallas Cowboys' Everson Walls, that is—couldn't bat the ball away. Dwight—San Francisco's Dwight Clark—did catch Joe Montana's high throw in the back of the end zone. The touchdown gave the San Francisco 49ers a 28–27 victory over the Dallas Cowboys, the NFC Championship, and the team's first trip to the Super Bowl. It also proved the effectiveness of Bill Walsh's revolutionary system, the West Coast Offense.

THE FOUNDATION FOR A SUPER BOWL MARRIAGE

Over the course of the dating and engagement process, a couple will often say, "I love you." They will say it publicly during the wedding ceremony. Everyone will hear it and likely take it for granted, recognizing it as perfunctory "wedding speak." What man and woman would get married and not speak of love? And what husband would not insist, "Of course I love my wife. I loved her when we got married, and I still love her!" Who doesn't believe he or she knows what love means? How could we not? We say it often. We hear about it all the time.

Television and movies often portray love as a powerful feeling. People fall in love, but the feeling eventually dulls. People fall out of love. It's part of a natural progression. The time comes to move on. Maybe fall in love again.

And sex is frequently part of this popular image. Sometimes as the bonding act of two people who have fallen in love. Sometimes as the catalyst for two people starting the process.

Love was not a powerful-but-temporary feeling to the apostle Paul. It was anything but status quo. It wasn't about sex. And it certainly wasn't a wedding cliché. He was not numb to love. It was fresh to him.

"I want to make sure we're talking about the same thing," Paul might say if he was talking to each of us about love. He might drape an arm across our shoulders or put a finger in our chests. "Forget what you know or think you know. Let's start all over with the idea of love. We're going to redefine it, and it is going to redefine us. It is going to pervade everything we do!"

> Love is patient, love is kind. It does not envy, it does
> not boast, it is not proud. It is not rude, it is not self-
> seeking, it is not easily angered, it keeps no record of
> wrongs. Love does not delight in evil but rejoices with
> the truth. It always protects, always trusts, always
> hopes, always perseveres. Love never fails. (1 Corin-
> thians 13:4–8)

A husband commits to love his wife. We think we know what we're saying. After all, it's love. But here's a little different approach. Go through that 1 Corinthians passage and replace the word *love* with your name. Reads a little differently, doesn't it? Now comes the hard part, at least for me: to live it.

"Serve one another in love," says Galatians 5:13—another wedding cliché, unless you stop to think about what it should mean to each of us. Again, Paul might pull us aside and say, "Now that we're on the same page about love, let's talk about serving. Let's talk about putting your wife's well-being ahead of your own. Not just a single act or for only a day, a month, or even a year. How about as a way of life?"

What if I'm tired and just don't feel like giving to the relationship? Persevere in your marriage, the way Christ would.

What if my wife is stuck in her own issues? Be patient in your marriage, the way Jesus would.

What if I meet someone and begin to wonder if I made the right choice? Protect your marriage, the way Christ would.

What happens when I start to wonder, "What's in this whole 'Serve one another in love' thing for me?" Trust in the system, the way Jesus would.

What if we have an argument and she says things that hurt or embarrass me? Talk about it but keep no records of wrong, the way Jesus would.

It's only over time that a husband can begin to realize what a challenge 1 Corinthians 13 is. Life is challenging. But serving someone in love for a lifetime? Way challenging. And if we start measuring what we think we're putting into our marriages against what we think we're getting out of them, we may not have bought into love the way we think we have. If we don't challenge ourselves every day to that standard of excellence, we're holding out on our teammates.

It's also only over time that we experience the rewards of having a marriage that is lived in this way. But we have to have faith in this system of love. We may not see the results we'd like for a while.

Paul defined faith as being "sure of what we hope for and certain of what we do not see" (Hebrews 11:1). Coach Walsh had faith. He was sure of what he hoped for. Certain of what he could not see? Maybe. At least he was certain of what he *believed* he could see.

Every coach knows he has to get the buy-in from the players. Whether they verbalize it or not, what the players want to know, what they need to know, is "What's in it for me? If I do what you're asking me to do, will I get what's most important to me?" Man or woman, young or old, the thing that is most important to all people is strong, intimate connection. It's companionship on a whole different level. It's love, and we were made with a need to both give and receive it. To know another and be known by another. To know we are deeply cared about and to deeply care about someone else. It happens on great teams, and it happens on great marriage teams.

It was not good that man was alone (see Genesis 2:18). Christ promised us that we could have that kind of connection, but we have to do it His way, the 1 Corinthians 13 way.

Accepting Walsh's unproven West Coast Offense in 1979 was an act of faith. But really, what did a 2-14 team have to lose? Sticking with it a second season, after another 2-14 record, might have been a truer test of faith. But accepting it in 1989, after three Super Bowls? A person would have been crazy not to. It was obvious. At least it was obvious to George Seifert, the man who succeeded Walsh and became the only first-year head coach to lead a defending Super Bowl champion to a repeat. And to prove he wasn't just riding the coattails of Walsh and Joe Montana, Seifert won it all again five years later with Steve Young as his quarterback.

First Corinthians 13 is an overarching relationship philosophy. It's a framework strong enough to withstand the shocks of life. But it's also flexible enough to adapt to change. It's comprehensive enough to inspire a big-picture perspective. And it's specific enough to apply to every aspect of life. It's so challenging that it can never be fully achieved. Yet the successes we do experience are so rewarding that we never should stop trying.

"When I think of Bill Walsh and the 'West Coast Offense,' I think less of the actual X's and O's than I do of the comprehensive approach Coach Walsh took to creating a structure," says the Baltimore Ravens' Brian Billick, once an assistant under Walsh. A different approach.

First Corinthians 13 love was a different approach in Paul's day. And it's a different approach now. It creates an environment that allows and encourages you and your wife to become all that God made each of you to be. The marriage partners you can be. The parenting partners you can be. The marketplace people you can be.

A Super Bowl marriage will take time. It will take commitment. And it will take trust in the system. You may be just starting your marriage with hopes of first making the playoffs. After that, the Super Bowl. Or you may be wondering if you can turn around a twenty-year relationship that is 2-14. The great teams have confidence. But before that, they have faith. If you don't act on faith in the love and servanthood way explained by 1 Corinthians 13 and

Galatians 5:13, you won't develop the confidence necessary to achieve a Super Bowl marriage.

The Extra Point

The man with the full head of white hair enters the room for his first talk to his new team. Bill Walsh moves to the front of the room and scans the team, nodding approvingly.

"Gentlemen, I believe in you," he begins. "And I believe in this offensive system. With you men in this system, there is no limit to what we can accomplish. You probably don't believe that, but it's true. But I need your hearts. I need your commitment. This system will work, but you have to make it work. And it's going to take time to see the results. Our goal is not improvement. We all will improve. But improvement is just steps along the way. Our goal is winning the Super Bowl."

What does this guy know? you wonder. *The Packers dominated the sixties by running the ball down people's throats. The Steelers dominated the seventies by Bradshaw's throwing deep to Swann and Stallworth, and Bleier and Harris pounding the ball. I don't know if this can work.*

"I can't make you believe. You have three choices," continues Walsh. "You can pack up and get out now. You can go through the motions till we find somebody who will believe and pay the price to win. Or you can be that person who believes, pays the price, and enjoys the fruits of our successes. You decide."

———

Go through 1 Corinthians 13:4–8 and insert your name where the word *love* appears. Now, beginning with just one aspect of your marriage, apply that approach to your relationship.

winning isn't everything

I was involved in football, as a player and a coach,
for forty years and never had a philosophy other than
"Whip the other guy." People sometimes make
the game more complicated than it is.

—MIKE DITKA

T he clock was stopped. The teams readied themselves for the play that would determine the winner of the closest Super Bowl ever played. In eight short seconds, one of these conference champions would walk off the field a winner and one a loser. It is the cruel efficiency of football that the efforts of an entire season can sometimes hinge on a single play. Fair? Maybe not, but those are the rules everyone plays by.

Coming into the game, the AFC team was peaking. Maybe they should have tried invoking precedence and momentum. Perhaps they could have been declared the winner of this duel without a single shot being fired. The two teams had met in the fifteenth game of the regular season, a contest the AFC team had won 17–13.

Two weeks later they scored on eight possessions to win a 44–34 shootout in the first round of the playoffs. They swamped their opponents with 41 first-half points in a 51–3 blowout the following week in the conference championship game. They were on a playoff roll. Those considerations obviously influenced the oddsmakers when they made the team 7-point favorites going into the game. Previous games, even previous playoff games, are of no consequence in the Super Bowl, however.

The NFC team could have attempted a sentimental appeal. Their starting quarterback, the conference's leading passer, had been injured in the week-fifteen defeat and had been lost for the remainder of the season, including the playoffs. His long-on-years, short-on-experience backup would lead the offense. He had thrown no passes in his first four seasons and only sixty-eight in the next two combined. He had spent most of the current season, his seventh, carrying a clipboard until the late-season injury to the starter. If a game could be decided solely on positive emotional feelings for the underdog, the NFC would have been declared the winner prior to kickoff. Human-interest stories are exactly that, however—merely interesting. They don't decide winners.

Of course, it would have been hard to work up much of an underdog sentiment for the NFC team. They had finished the regular season with a 13-3 record. In the first round of the playoffs, they had gone on the road to grind out a 15–13 win over the defending Super Bowl champions, a team favored to three-peat. The offense was a conservative, pounding unit that turned the ball over only fourteen times, setting a record for the lowest turnover rate in a sea-son. They didn't need a gunslinger quarterback. Their defense was a physical bunch, coached by a thirty-eight-year-old *wunderkind,* who today is considered the best head coach in the NFL. The defense was led by one of the most disruptive linebackers ever to blindside a quarterback, a player offensive coordinators had to plan the game around. They had allowed the fewest points in the league. The head coach had already won a Super Bowl and was acknowl-edged as one of the game's best. Underdogs, maybe, but it wasn't exactly Pharaoh's army versus the Red Sea.

The AFC team could have appealed to have the game decided by individual excellence. They sent ten players to the Pro Bowl, while the NFC team sent only seven. However, individual perfor-mance during the regular season is what qualifies a player for the Pro Bowl. Though a high number of Pro Bowl players suggests that a team will do well, it doesn't ensure a Super Bowl championship.

The NFC team could have attempted to halt the game after they kicked a field goal on their opening drive, the first score of the game. The odds were in their favor at that point. The team that had scored first had won seventeen of the previous twenty-four Super Bowls. The AFC could have lobbied to wrap it up at half, when they were ahead 12–10 by virtue of a safety. Eighteen of the previ-ous Super Bowl winners had been ahead at halftime, and all three of the teams that had recorded safeties in earlier Super Bowls had come out on top. As the statistics imply, scoring first and holding a lead at the half are important, but they are only points along the way.

The NFC team could have attempted to have the game decided by dominating execution of a brilliant game plan. The offense had ground it out, and the defense had hammered away. True to their conservative approach and to the delight of their coach, they had set a Super Bowl record by holding on to the ball for over forty minutes—including a Super Bowl record nine-minute, twenty-nine-second drive. Their high-powered opponents couldn't score if they didn't have the ball. When they did have the ball, they had been confounded by a defense that primarily played two down linemen, supplemented by blitzing linebackers, and big defensive backs, who pounded the receivers.

The strategy of the NFC tortoise had been as effective (386 yards in forty minutes, twenty-nine seconds of possession en route to 20 points) as the AFC hare (371 yards in nineteen minutes, twenty-three seconds for 19 points). The stories had played themselves out. The statistics had been compiled. None of that mattered, however. Not time of possession, score-by-quarter breakdowns, efficient execution of a sound game plan, number of Pro Bowl players, prior game results, hype, reputation, or sentimental appeal.

There is never any doubt about the winner of the Super Bowl. The game is played in accordance with a small book entitled *Official Rules of the NFL* in which section 1, article 1 of rule 11 clearly states, "The team that scores the greater number of points during the entire game is the winner." And unlike regular season games, in which there can be a tie, playoff games continue until one team has met that single, simple criterion.

With the clock reading eight seconds, the AFC coach sent his field-goal team onto the field for a 47-yard attempt, hoping to become the first team in seven years from that conference to win the Super Bowl. The kicker had never made one from that distance on grass, but championship games are often the stage for unprecedented accomplishment.

The snap was good. The hold was sure. The offensive line did its job. The kick cleared all the outstretched hands at the line of scrimmage and sailed through the Tampa sky. The title of World Champions was literally up in the air, tumbling end over end toward the goalposts. As the ball tumbled through the sky, it began to fade to the right. New York Giants players began thrusting their arms skyward in celebration even as Buffalo Bills players were hanging their heads in disappointment. Pepper Johnson had commandeered the cooler of Gatorade and was snaking through his teammates for the customary dousing of Giants' head coach Bill Parcells.

Jeff Hostetler, the career backup quarterback, turned in an efficient, mistake-free twenty for thirty-two performance. Venerable running back O. J. Anderson earned MVP honors with 102 yards in twenty-one carries behind his massive offensive line. Bill Belichick coordinated the efforts of Lawrence Taylor and his defensive mates as they throttled Buffalo's No-Huddle Offense.

At 0:00 the stadium scoreboard made it official. The New York Giants had defeated the Buffalo Bills 20–19 to win the twenty-fifth Super Bowl. Once again "the team that scores the greater number of points during the entire game" was declared the winner. It is the one simple thing all Super Bowls have had in common.

Winning the Marriage Game

The winning team in football is the one that scores the most points in the game. How does a couple determine if they are on a winning marriage team? What standard can they point to and say, "We are winning the marriage game because…"?

How about simply staying married? With so many couples divorcing, shouldn't preserving the union count for something? It does count for something. It means you keep showing up for the game. Staying together is the marriage equivalent of catching the team bus to the stadium. It is necessary.

Merely staying married doesn't mean a husband and wife have a successful relationship, though. Many couples stay married but simply go through the motions. They never specifically talk about what they want their marriage to look like. Maybe they don't agree on where they want the relationship to go. Or perhaps they talk about it and agree on it, but they don't take the necessary steps as a team to make it happen. They simply bump along through life, settling for what is comfortable. They give what they feel like giving or know how to give, and they hope it will be enough to keep things together. They don't grow, and neither does their marriage.

No, staying married is not the standard against which successful marriages should be measured.

Most married couples decide to have children, and they are a wonderful addition to the family. Parents invest themselves in the demanding task of developing another human being. They want their children to have good friends and to do well in school. They want them to be involved in the extracurricular activities that will help them have fun and explore different aspects of their personalities, skills, and interests. Parents go to great lengths and make innumerable sacrifices to provide a loving, supportive environment for their children, hoping they will one day have satisfying adult lives of their own.

Children have a tremendous impact on their parents' marriage, and the parents' marriage will have a tremendous effect on their children. But whether children disappoint their parents or exceed their wildest dreams, they are not the standard by which the success of a marriage should be determined.

Some couples who desperately want children are unable to conceive, or they miscarry prior to birth. Some children are born with mental or physical conditions that dramatically change a couple's paradigm of parenthood and make a "normal" life impossible. Though the parent-child relationship typically continues throughout the lives of the parents and their children, the consuming project of child rearing comes to an end. And the dynamics change as our children become adults.

Some couples will go through marriage acting as though the lifestyle they achieve is the standard by which their relationship will be judged. They may invest a great deal of energy in being socially active. One or both spouses may work diligently in challenging marketplace positions and achieve commensurate financial rewards. They may have an address that causes people to nod their heads in approval, take enviable vacations, drive cars that enclose them in hushed elegance, and send their children to the finest schools in the country.

None of these things are bad, unless they are used to measure the success of the relationship.

What about happiness? When you strip away all other considerations, isn't the happiness of a husband and wife what really matters? "As long as we're happy…" Happiness is not a bad thing, but it shouldn't be a goal. If it is, we may become more concerned about the approval of our wives instead of their true well-being. And if we're happy where we are as a couple, we may not have the energy and courage to do what's necessary to keep moving ahead in the relationship. The "happiness" standard is often a disguise for complacency and fear.

The number of years together, "how the kids turn out" (whatever that means), success in business and the lifestyle it affords, and some vague sense of happiness are all ways that people commonly, if not consciously, measure the quality of their marriages.

Our lives can get pretty complicated. And our marriages can become just one more ball we're trying to juggle. Perhaps just another thing that…well, if we're not doing it poorly, it must be okay.

But doing okay isn't what God had in mind for us, in life or marriage.

"Whatever you do, work at it with all your heart, as working for the Lord, not for men," Paul exhorts in Colossians 3:23. He encourages us to "live a life worthy of the Lord and…please him in every way" (Colossians 1:10) and to "serve wholeheartedly, as if you were serving the Lord, not men" (Ephesians 6:7). It seems Paul was more concerned about excellence than doing okay.

So is there a standard by which we should judge the success of a marriage?

The Lombardi Trophy, awarded to the winner of the Super Bowl, is named for Vince Lombardi, the coach of the legendary Green Bay Packers of the 1960s. They were one of the best teams of all time, maybe *the* best, but during one four-game stretch in 1965, the Packers scored a total of three touchdowns. Though his defense won two of those games for him, Lombardi had had enough. His background was offense. His signature play was a ruthlessly efficient "here-it-comes, stop-us-if-you-can" power sweep. His team was loaded with All Pros and future Hall of Famers, but they couldn't score. He decided it was time for a little chat with the boys.

"He was furious," recalled one of the players. "He told us to forget everything he'd told us, to scrap it all, that we were going back to the basics and fundamentals. He reached down and picked up a football and said, with that great sarcastic grin, 'This is a football.'"

It must have worked. The Packers averaged 28 points a game the remainder of the season, a season that concluded with a victory over Cleveland in the last NFL championship game before the Super Bowl era.

What if God's *primary* desire for marriage, His simplest let's-go-back-to-the-basics purpose for the relationship, was not duration of the relationship, kids, careers, lifestyle, or happiness? What if God's primary purpose for marriage is that it would make us more like Jesus? Could it really be that simple?

Christlikeness is a standard so challenging that we can never reach it. But it's a vision so compelling that we can never stop reaching for it. Like Christ Himself, it attracts rather than intimidates. It can be pursued with relentless single-mindedness because its focus is not narrow and self-absorbed. It's not the kind of single-mindedness that isolates us from other people, including our spouses. It's the kind of focus that leads to true connection with others, especially our wives. It's so comprehensive that it can be applied to all aspects of marriage and life. It's so simple and clear that we can always say either, "I'm moving toward the goal" or "I'm moving away from the goal." If we're honest.

It's what we were made for, in life and in marriage.

We'll never get there, but marriage is an effective tool in our ongoing transformation. Marriage is where we will most regularly face the choice of serving ourselves or serving others. And it is a game we play every day, regardless of whether we want to or not.

So what was Jesus like?

He was the teammate you always wanted to play with and the One you always wanted to be like. He was strong, purposeful, selfless, and tough. Oh my, was He tough! Take one for the team? I'd say He did. Got your back? You bet He did. There for His team-mates? You know He was. Even when they weren't there for Him.

He saw potential, not limitations. He was an optimistic builder of people who was passionately committed to helping others become what He knew they could be, even if they didn't know. He accepted people where they were but didn't let them take the easy way out when their character was at stake, especially when He knew they'd need that toughness down the road. He inspired but did not demand. He was resourceful and did whatever it took to move His team ahead. His unshakable confidence in Himself infected those on His team. Losing was not an option. But when they came up short, He didn't give up on them. His whole life was about winning the relationship game.

That may not be how you think of Jesus. But if you really examine His life, those qualities are obvious. Too often people settle for what we think are the dos and don'ts of the religion of Christ instead of acquiring His attitude and character.

He was the personification of 1 Corinthians 13. He was every-thing that love really is, not what we have confined it to or what we want to believe it is. That is our standard. First Corinthians 13 is both our means to the end and the end itself.

"Am I becoming more patient in my marriage?" I am ripping off first downs if I am.

"Am I getting better at recognizing areas of conflict, initiating calm discussions about them, working on solutions, and forgiving failures?" If I can honestly say I am growing in these areas, I am mounting a long drive in the marriage game.

"Am I becoming more hopeful about our relationship, more trusting in my partner, and more determined to keep trying even when I fail?" If I am piling up those points, I am winning the game.

"Am I becoming less self-seeking and more concerned about the needs of my spouse?" If the answer is yes, I am winning the game.

Scott Norwood's attempted field goal was wide to the right in Super Bowl XXV, and the Giants won the game. There were no illusions about anything else really mattering. "The team that scores the greater number of points during the entire game is the winner."

"Winning isn't everything. It's the only thing" is a quote often attributed to Lombardi. He was right. It's the kind of consuming singleness of purpose required to succeed, especially when the game is marriage.

Becoming more like Christ isn't everything. It's the only thing. There is never any doubt about who will win the marriage game. It's the man who accepts the challenge of becoming like Jesus and commits himself to success on the playing field of marriage.

The Extra Point

"Okay, in a minute we hit the field," Parcells tells you. "This is it. This is what all that practice is about. Offense, we're counting on you to put up some points. We need this one."

You head out of the tunnel onto the beautifully trimmed green grass into the sunshine and the roar of the crowd.

You notice something's not right, but it doesn't hit you right away. Then you stop. No hash marks, no yard markers, no sidelines, no end zones. Just a huge oval of grass in front of seventy thousand fans. No first-down chains. No goalposts. No scoreboard. No clock. No way of directing your energy into purposeful activity. A tough way to play the game.

"Come on," says the official.

"Where are the goalposts?"

"Don't need 'em. Come on."

"But how will we know…"

"Let's go! Just play the game."

———

How do you measure the level of success in your marriage?

Would you say you're winning or losing?

THE I IN TEAM

*The veterans on this defense…tell me, "I need you
to be a man." So I never want them to look at me,
ever, and say I wasn't a man.*

—LaVar Arrington

He had a devastating influence. He was just unrelenting.
He refused to lose. And he made huge plays when they
had to be made.… He was just an awesome addition to our squad.
He just hated to lose. He hated to get beat," said the seventh-year
linebacker, reflecting on the impact of his rookie teammate, the
fourth player taken in the 1969 draft. "And he just refused to accept
that we were losers. He was unquestionably the player of the decade.
There was no player who was more valuable to his team."

How the "awesome addition" could not arrive at the conclusion
that he had joined a team of losers is a mystery. Though they would
one day become arguably the best NFL team ever, they were undis-
putedly the worst in 1968. They had not had a winning season since
1963, losing forty-nine of the sixty-nine games they played during
that five-year stretch. Their 2-11-1 record in 1968 was their second

two-win season of the sixties. On offense only three teams scored fewer points. And on defense no team allowed more. They stunk on both sides of the ball. If the Hall of Fame had a wing devoted to wishful thinkers, the rookie would have been a unanimous choice.

The rookie defensive tackle was more than a first-round draft pick. He was the first player drafted by the first-year coach, a symbolic start of a new era. He was also the cornerstone upon which the coach hoped to build a defense and a team. Nine rounds later the team selected another defensive lineman, an end out of Arkansas–Pine Bluff. Together the linebacker, his rookie defensive mates, the new coach, and the rest of the team began the task of rebuilding.

With nowhere to go but up, they actually went down. Of course from 2-11-1 it couldn't get a lot worse, and the upside of their 1-13 season was another college draft in which they again selected early in each round. With the first pick in the third round, they grabbed a big, physical cornerback out of Southern University whose eventual mastery of bump-and-run coverage caused a change in the rules, and looked ahead to the next year.

In 1970 they showed signs of resurgence and finished 5-9. In the spring of '71 they drafted a linebacker, two defensive linemen, and a safety. They also signed a rookie free agent safety. A defensive unit was beginning to take shape. Though the team was improving, their record climbed to only 6-8 in the fall of that year. Call it purposeful patience.

"There was a frustration among the players because they were trying to achieve what we wanted and many times came close," explained the coach. "The big danger was avoiding any finger-pointing. We told them that if anyone was going to point a finger, point it at the mirror. We said the attitude has to be 'If we are not winning, it is my fault.' With that attitude, everything else falls into place."

The defensive line puzzle was completed in 1972 when a defensive tackle came off the taxi squad to alternate as a starter. The team shed their losers' image that year as they won their division with an 11-3 record and qualified for the playoffs.

The most famous and controversial play in the history of the NFL carried them to a first-round playoff victory that year. The following week they lost by 4 points in the conference championship game to the eventual Super Bowl winners and the only undefeated team in NFL history. They'd come a long way since that abysmal 1-13 in '69, but they weren't yet where they needed to be.

In the spring of 1973 they added a cornerback to the defense, and expectations rose. That season proved to be a disappointment, however. Their record dropped to 10-4, and they were thumped 33–14 in the first round of the playoffs by the team they had beaten in the playoffs the year before.

They may have drafted "the player of the decade" in '69, but it was their '74 draft that was the league's best ever. They added a center, who would appear in nine Pro Bowls during his Hall of Fame career, and two receivers, who together would total seven Pro Bowls and two Hall of Fame inductions. They also took a chance in the second round on a six-foot-four, 220-pound middle linebacker out of Kent State.

The final piece of the defense was locked in. The rebuilding, begun in 1969, was now complete. Position by position, draft by draft, the defense had been built. Game by game, season by season, the individual players had become an integrated unit. And that integrated unit gave up only 189 points in 1974, by far the fewest points in the AFC.

"Becoming a winner is a day-to-day thing, teaching, learning and growing," said the coach. "A team must grow together and does not grow immediately." That patience was rewarded with a victory in Super Bowl IX in which they allowed their opponents only 17 rushing yards and a total of 119 yards en route to a 16–6 victory.

The team improved to a league-best 12-2 in 1975. It was the second full year in which all the defensive starters played together. As good as they had been before, they got even better, surrendering only 162 points on their way to winning a second consecutive Super Bowl. It looked like a dynasty had emerged.

The year 1976 showed how quickly things can change, however. They went from world champions to losing four of their first five games. The proud and physical defense gave up an average of 21 points in the first five games, including 31 in the season opener and 30 in the third game. Oops, looks like everyone was wrong about the dynasty thing.

Then, just as quickly, things changed again. The defense began an unprecedented string of dominant performances. In the next nine games of 1976 the defense allowed a *total* of 38 points, an average of 4 a game. That run of excellence included five shutouts.

The NFL's other twenty-seven teams *combined* recorded only seventeen shutouts, and no other team had more than two. After giving up *at least* two touchdowns in four of those first five games, the team allowed *only* two touchdowns in the entire remaining nine games.

They were ready for the playoffs and thrashed their first-round opponent 40–14. That victory proved costly, however. They became the first team to have two 1,000-yard rushers in the same season, and both were hurt in the rout. Those injuries proved fatal to the team's hopes for a third consecutive Super Bowl championship. Unable to mount an offense against their old nemesis, the 13-1 Oakland Raiders, they fell 24–7 in the AFC championship game. Though they won their division the following season, their 9-5 record was the worst in six years, and they lost in the first round of the playoffs, giving up 20 second-half points.

Great teams make adjustments and get back on track. Their commitment doesn't waver, and they don't lower the standard. The following year this team concluded the regular season with a 14-2 record and the postseason with a 35–31 victory in the Super Bowl. And the next season they once again defended their championship to become the only team to twice win back-to-back Super Bowls.

By winning four Super Bowls in six years, Chuck Noll's Pittsburgh Steelers proved that the label of "dynasty," though premature in 1976, was justified. Is it possible we'd be talking about five championships in six years if Franco Harris, the hero of the Immaculate Reception, and Rocky Bleier, his fellow thousand-yard rusher, had not been injured in the '76 playoffs? We'll never know. We do know that no team, before or since, has demonstrated such sustained dominance.

In fact, we'll never again see a team as dominant as the '70s Steelers. Why? Because you'll never again see that number of players with that level of skills stay together for that long. Not in today's free-agent NFL. The starters on that Steelers team totaled 122 NFL seasons among them. One hundred and sixteen were as Steelers. Of those eleven starters, eight played their entire careers in the black and gold of Pittsburgh, including Joe Greene, the cornerstone laid in the '69 draft, and Jack Lambert, the skinny middle linebacker from Kent State who completed the puzzle in '74. Seven of the eleven went to the Pro Bowl that year, and four are in the Hall of Fame. Good team? Scary good.

The Marriage Team

The wheels were starting to wobble. The pressure was mounting and so were the finger-pointing and carping. The team was in trouble.

"Hey, we're on the same team."

I stopped and looked at Tari. Stress outside of our relationship was getting to us, and we were going after each other. We were tense, impatient, and frustrated. The stress was not her fault or mine, but it was showing up in how we related to each other. She had the presence of mind to identify what was going on and call my attention to it. I realized she was right. We were on the same team.

It was a classic *aha!* moment. I had never thought of her as a teammate prior to that. A partner, yes. A teammate, no. I knew we planned to share life together, but it had not occurred to me that for our marriage to be a success, we would have to be a great team. I had played on teams before. I knew how to be a teammate. I loved the sense of contributing to something bigger than I was. This was just a different team. I would have to know what was expected of me and deliver. Tari would have to do the same. And what would be expected of us as marriage teammates?

"Each one of you also must love his wife as he loves himself," Paul insists in Ephesians 5:33, "and the wife must respect her husband." He gives a mutual, unconditional command. The reason Paul is so simple and specific could be that respect and love may be the most important needs in the marriage relationship. A husband's greatest need is to be respected, and a wife's greatest need is to be loved. It's that simple. Yes, a husband needs to feel loved, and a wife needs to feel respected, and each will have other needs as well, such as appreciation, encouragement, affection, approval, attention, comfort, and support.

The need for acceptance is huge for both husbands and wives. It's essential that we feel accepted by our spouses. Acceptance leads to a safe environment, and a safe environment allows us to be ourselves. Without acceptance we hide significant parts of ourselves— often our weaknesses, the parts of ourselves that need to be out in the open so we can address them. Without acceptance, our team will never be as strong as it needs to be to overcome the obstacles en route to a Super Bowl marriage. Unconditional love—that's the standard we're working to achieve. The kind of love Jesus demonstrated. The kind of love we often hear taught and discussed. First Corinthians 13 love.

But also unconditional respect. Husbands don't have to earn respect any more than wives have to earn love, says Emerson Eggerichs in his book *Love and Respect.* That's a message you don't hear a lot, and most likely it will require some time to consider. Take a closer look at the Ephesians 5 passage and see for yourself that Paul doesn't attach conditions to either love or respect. It might also help to look at how respectfully Jesus treated people, regardless of whether they were considered worthy of respect. Tax collectors, prostitutes, people who were crippled and lame—they hadn't earned His respect, yet that's what Jesus gave them. More than not having earned His respect, they conducted their lives in ways that could have brought His scorn. But that's not how He saw them. To Jesus, they were creations of God and therefore worthy of respect.

Why should a couple challenge themselves with unconditional love and respect? It's in their best interests to do so.

Biblical commands are not moral hoops to jump through on our way to earning God's favor. They're not some kind of random test God has devised to measure our worth. Biblical commands are God's instructions to us on how to have respectful, loving, and mutually beneficial relationships.

That's especially true in marriage. A man needs the respect of his wife to become the best possible husband he can be. And a woman needs the love of her husband to become the best possible wife she can be. When we do our job, it frees our wives to do theirs.

Unconditional respect comes as naturally to wives as unconditional love does to husbands, which is to say to live and relate this way is work. But that's okay. We care the most about the things in which we invest the most. A man needs to love his wife unconditionally. A wife needs to respect her husband unconditionally. It takes that kind of effort to win the marriage game.

Why wouldn't a couple rise to the challenge of unconditional love and respect? Fear. Plain and simple fear. We are afraid to be so nakedly dependent on another person to meet a need that only he or she can meet. In our darker moments we're also afraid if we meet their needs that we'll lose the leverage we need to make them change. We wonder, *If they're getting what they want and need, why would they change?*

As husbands, our focus should not be how our wives need to change. When we start focusing on how they need to change and what we can do to change them, we take our eyes off our own growth.

Instead, the focus for both husbands and wives should be growing to be more like Jesus. The marriage relationship is a significant part of that process. Receiving unconditional respect and love is not an excuse for self-serving, unrespectable, unloving, and un-Christlike behavior any more than grace is. As a matter of fact, spouses who say, "Well, she's supposed to respect me regardless" or

"He's supposed to love me regardless" ensure they will never move toward Christlikeness.

How committed do you have to be to give your spouse unconditional love and respect? Marital commitment is not a question of how much or how little. Marital commitment is a question of yes or no. Either you are committed or you aren't. If you are, you'll figure it out. If you're not, you'll figure out a way around it.

Attitude is contagious. Commitment to excellence and superior execution leads to stronger commitment and even better execution. Good teammates make one another better.

"I firmly believe that if I had played for the Tampa Bay Buccaneers I would not be in the Hall of Fame. The Hall of Fame is more a credit to our football team than it is to an individual," insists linebacker Jack Ham. The effectiveness of Ham's teammates contributed to his effectiveness. The same is true in marriage.

When a husband loves his wife as Jesus loved the church, and a wife respects her husband as Jesus respected people in His life, both feel more secure in the relationship and confident in themselves. He is inspired to stronger love; she feels a growing respect. His love becomes even stronger, as does her respect. Their confidence in each other grows, and their marriage team becomes an awesome unit. It is an upward spiral.

Unfortunately, the same is true with mediocrity and indifference. Teammates can make each other worse by a casual attitude about the team, sloppy execution, and a what's-in-it-for-me spirit.

It would be easy to attribute Pittsburgh's defensive dominance to individual brilliance. But to do so would be an injustice to the team, which took years to build, and an affront to the players who grew to know each other and their roles so well. Defensive tackle Joe Greene and cornerback Mel Blount excelled at their own positions. Neither could have done what the other did. Though the Steelers' pair of Jacks—Lambert and Ham—both played linebacker, one played the middle and one the outside. They excelled also, each at *his own* position. The individual defensive players became an excellent unit. The bottom line? Four Super Bowl championships in six years.

When you join a team, the needs of the team supersede your own. And when you join a marriage team, the needs of your spouse come before your own. If they don't, you could find yourself locked in something Eggerichs calls "the Crazy Cycle."

When a husband feels disrespected, he has a natural tendency to react in ways that feel unloving to his wife. When a wife feels unloved, she has a natural tendency to react in ways that feel disrespectful to her husband. Without love, she reacts without respect. Without respect, he reacts without love—ad nauseam.

A husband's bottom line? Create a relationship environment where his wife is secure in his love, certain of his passion to improve in his role as a husband, and inspired by his commitment to her and their marriage team. A wife's bottom line? Create a relationship environment in which her husband is secure in her respect for him, confident in her passion to improve as a wife, and certain of her commitment to the marriage team. He loves; she respects. She respects; he loves. It's what Eggerichs calls "the Energizing Cycle."

Chuck Noll encouraged his players to adopt the attitude "If we're not winning, it's my fault." It was his way of saying, "Take the log out of your own eye" (see Matthew 7:2–5). If you feel your partner is somehow falling short in her role, you must first ask yourself how you are measuring up as a mate. How effectively are you loving your wife? You are not solely responsible for the success of the marriage, but you are entirely responsible for your contribution. Contrary to the old coaching cliché, there is an "I" in team. *What do I have to do to move the team ahead? How can I contribute to the success of my teammate? How can I improve as a spouse? Am I consistently loving my wife in ways that she understands? Am I building a marriage environment in which she is secure?* And a wife has to go through the same process.

It takes time to build a strong marriage team, but not just time. It takes time in purposeful pursuit of an excellent marriage. Time while extending grace, support, encouragement, love, and respect to each other. Time in passionate pursuit of your own growth.

I no longer have a choice about whether or not I will be on a team. I made the choice when I married Tari. I joined a team. I became a husband and a teammate. The choice I now make every day is whether my approach to those roles is committed and focused or casual and distracted. My choices will determine the success of my team. Our life experiences are teaching her whether or not I will be there for her. Am I committed to growing as a husband? Am I the weak link on our team or a cornerstone upon whom she can count? If I become the husband I can be, she will become the wife I need. Confidence in your teammates frees you up to play the game with reckless abandon, but doubt infects a team with hesitation and fear.

"I felt sometimes when we needed a big play I could take a chance, but those chances were pretty calculated," said L. C. Greenwood, the tenth-round draft pick in '69 who played his entire thirteen-year career with Joe Greene at his side. "I could get out of the original defensive structure and make a play because I knew where Joe, Lambert and Ham would be."

I am never going to play in the Super Bowl. My big game is my marriage. If I make a mistake, Joe, Lambert, and Ham will not be there to cover for me. Tari will be there, however, and I will be there for her. We are building a marriage and a life together. We are a team. We've shared many experiences that have helped us grow in confidence and trust in each other, but we are not perfect. We've also dropped the ball and failed to execute. Sometimes for just one play. Sometimes for a whole season. But regardless of the circumstances or outcome, we are still a team, one that will be together the rest of our lives.

Good team? Yes, we are. And we have the potential to get better, but we also have the opportunity to get worse. Most likely we're not even at the half yet. There's a long way to go and a lot of adjustments we'll have to make.

Day by day, week by week, year by year, season of life by season of life, a husband and wife are about the business of building their marriage team. They are reinforcing the critical foundation of love and respect so that each can become a better spouse, a better parent, a better person in the marketplace—whatever roles they find themselves in. The choice we face is whether we are committed to paying the price to be a consistent Super Bowl marriage team or just another couple going through the motions and hoping things will work out.

The Extra Point

You're the second guy in the locker room before the conference championship against the Raiders. Joe Greene is the first, and he walks over to you.

"This is a gang fight, a war. If we're going to win, you have to come through. I'm counting on you. You know what you have to do. And I know you can do it. Will you?" He needs to know.

"Okay, I'll try."

"Try? I'm going to be banging against Gene Upshaw and Art Shell all day. And we're going to chase Ken Stabler around back there. But I have to know you're going to cover those receivers. I can't do that. You have to, man."

He reaches out, grabs your shoulder, and fixes you with a stare. "Try?"

———

If your primary responsibility is making sure your wife is confident of your commitment to the marriage and feels secure in your love for her, how well are you doing your job?

Do you think your wife sees you as a teammate with a strong sense of the *I* in team?

The New Guy in the Middle

I'm starting to think after eighteen years in this league
that winning isn't so much overcoming your opponents.
It's overcoming yourself.

—BRUCE MATTHEWS

otential? How would you like to predict what might come to pass?

Speed? His 4.6 in the 40-yard dash was .2 seconds faster than the average for other players at this position taken in the previous year's draft. Fearless? He returned punts and kickoffs. Elusive? He did well enough to have qualified as the number eight punt returner in the country if he had returned only four more. Clutch performer? Of his seven receptions in his senior year, six were for touchdowns.

Versatile? In a four-year college career, he played tight end, wide receiver, safety, and linebacker. Stamina? He was on the field for a hundred snaps in a game his senior season. Relentless? In that game he was credited with twenty tackles, two fumble recoveries—including one he returned 71 yards for the touchdown that won the game—two deflected passes, and the recovery of an onside kick to ensure the victory. Dominating? He had led the nation with 178 tackles in his junior year.

Of course, in college he often wasn't blocked. "Every once in a while I'd get a receiver or a tight end, but most of the time I just ran free to the ball" is how he recalled his college days. "Every once in a while if I was blitzing, a lineman might block me. Usually nobody. It was easy; just go make a play." Easy or not, he had all the tools.

"This combination of size, speed, strength, smarts, character, maturity, throwback toughness, athletic ability, cover skills, and hands just doesn't come along very often" is how one scout described him.

The only knock was his collegiate pedigree. New Mexico isn't exactly Oklahoma or Florida State. That didn't stop an NFC Central team from taking him with the ninth pick in the draft or the coach from immediately announcing that he would be the starting strong-side linebacker. He was a special talent, and they wanted him in the game.

"We thought he'd grow into some things, but he's already doing some of them" was the assessment of the defensive coordinator after training camp had opened. "He's got good instincts and he knows how to find the football." The rookie was fulfilling his promise.

Three weeks later, however, the bloom was off the rose. "He still has far too many alignment and assignment mistakes," said the coordinator. "I know we've thrown a lot at him, but if you're going to be a starter in this league, you've got to perform like a starter. He's got to step up and reduce his errors."

"I knew it was going to be an adjustment, but it is faster than I thought," said the rookie. "The linemen are so much better than I'm used to from college.... Here there's always someone blocking me and I have to get used to getting off the blocks."

Ah, college—the good old days. His carefree, all-American, run-to-the-ball-and-pop-somebody days. His opponents were bigger now. They were also faster and stronger. A week later he was out as the starter. "I just don't have any technique," admitted the linebacker. "I need to work on my technique, hands and feet mostly. I've got to get those down, figure out what I'm doing."

Figure out what he's doing? Excuse me? First-round draft pick, a five-million-dollar signing bonus, and he's got to start figuring out what he's doing? A game he had played his whole life was now a mystery to him. His natural athleticism and the skills he had learned along the way weren't getting the job done anymore. He was overwhelmed. His weaknesses had been exposed, and there was no place to hide.

He started the season on the bench. He got some playing time, though, and was credited with five tackles and one assist in his first two games. He made the most of the shots he got and continued to work and learn in practice. Injuries to others gave him his break, and he was named a starter at middle linebacker for the third game.

He was the new guy in the middle, and he stepped into some long shadows. Three different middle linebackers that had preceded him in his team's long history were in the Hall of Fame, including the man often credited with pioneering the position and the one generally considered the fiercest of them all.

He had an idea what he'd see. He had watched a lot of film and listened to his coaches. He knew the offense would try to confuse him. He could count on some shifting and probably man in motion. He knew they'd run some play fakes, too. It's the same stuff every defender sees, but as a rookie he was more prone to confusion, less likely to identify plays and respond immediately.

He didn't have to wait long. He got in on his first tackle with an assist on the game's fourth play and another on the next play. His defense allowed an eight-play drive for a score on the opening possession. He got one tackle in the next series and four on the following possession. He looked as though he knew what was going on. He was flying to the ball.

His opponents were just as big, strong, and fast as the ones who had been confusing him only a few weeks ago. They were still on him as quickly, but his technique was becoming more second nature and less a matter of thought. He was identifying more quickly what his opponent was up to and was responding.

Late in the third quarter he showed just how far he'd come. With first-and-ten and the ball on his own 21-yard line, he saw a receiver go in motion to his left. At the snap of the ball, he saw the quarterback roll to his left also. A running back sneaked out to the right, along with the tackle, guard, and center, and the rookie had them on his radar. Was he seeing a play to his left or a screen to his right? He stayed home until he had a flash of recognition. When the quarterback stopped his roll to the left and turned back toward the right, the linebacker took off. He was on the move before the ball was in the air.

A screen pass. His analysis was correct, his angle of pursuit true. He scraped off the block of the 290-pound tackle and wrapped the running back up for a 4-yard loss. It was just a one play, but it removed any lingering doubts about whether he had the mental and physical ability to make it in the NFL.

In his first career start, Brian Urlacher of the Chicago Bears finished with a team high thirteen tackles, including two for losses, and one sack, in a 14–7 loss to the New York Giants.

"It definitely wasn't easy," said the rookie. "I just have to learn what I'm doing out there and try to get exactly where I'm supposed to go all the time. That's going to come with playing."

It was only one game, but he was catching on. It was a good beginning. He finished the season as the team's leading tackler and was named the NFC Defensive Rookie of the Year. It was only one season, but he had shown that all his potential might someday earn him a place alongside Bill George, Dick Butkus, and Mike Singletary, not only as the man in the middle for the Bears, but perhaps a man from the middle in the Hall of Fame.

The size of his opponents, the strength of his opponents, the speed of his opponents, how quickly plays develop—as Brian Urlacher found out, it's different in the NFL. Same game, different level of competition. Most college players—even good ones—don't make the transition.

A New Game Against an Old Foe

A lot of couples who seem to have good dating relationships don't make the transition to successful marriages. No reasonable newlywed enters the marriage game with the belief that his union is going to be an uninterrupted flow of bliss. Even rookie spouses know there will be ups and downs. Yet many marriages end in divorce. The team splits up. Other marriages stay together but never play at the Super Bowl level. The relationship may exist forever as an 8-8 team or worse, and always out of the playoffs.

Why?

Unlike the players in the NFL, many spouses consistently fail to identify the opponent. And many spouses who do identify him underestimate his abilities. We are surprised by his speed and how quickly he is on top of us. Once we're tied up with him, we are shocked at how strong he is. A powerful combination of quickness and strength. And smart? Whatever our weakness, he'll find it and exploit it. When we make adjustments to counter his game, he changes it. He's got the energy of a rookie and the resourcefulness of a ten-year veteran. But the defining characteristic of this opponent is his relentless determination to win. You may beat him and beat him and beat him, but he'll continue getting up and coming after you. You don't have to like him, but you have to respect him.

Our opponent is not the world around us. It's a tough place to play the game, but it's merely a distraction. Our primary opponent is not our spouse, though many of us may come to see our partner more as an adversary than a teammate. Our opponent is our own self-centeredness, our natural inclination to think first of ourselves.

We want to have a successful marriage, but there's a problem. We want to have it in ways that are easiest for us, ways that don't require more than we want to give. Self-centeredness, self-interest, self-orientation, selfishness—they're all variations of the same theme.

My marriage has helped me see, with inescapable clarity, just how quickly and naturally I think of myself. *How does this circumstance affect me? What will I have to do or give up? If I do this for Tari, can I cut a relationship corner somewhere else? What's the least I can give right now and get away with it? What does this action entitle me to?* Nothing shows me how un-Christlike I can be as frequently and deeply as my marriage. It used to surprise me. It doesn't anymore. I'm a twelve-year marriage veteran, and I know what to expect. Looking back, I can see that it's a pattern so consistent and deeply rooted that I can't remember a time it wasn't there.

Anyone who has raised a child knows how naturally we come by our self-centeredness. From our insistence on having things our own way to a clutching possessiveness of things that are "Mine!" the self-centeredness of children shows up in many ways. We are at the center of the universe, and everything is evaluated in terms of how it affects us. It's easy to recognize in children. It's easy to recognize in other adults. Not so easy to recognize in ourselves.

Paul gives his eloquent and challenging definition of love in 1 Corinthians 13. In that same chapter he also discusses the need to grow up emotionally, not just chronologically. "When I was a child,

I talked like a child, I thought like a child, I reasoned like a child," Paul says. "When I became a man, I put childish ways behind me" (verse 11). If self-centeredness is one of the distinguishing characteristics of children's behavior, the ability to love in a 1 Corinthians 13 way is a distinguishing characteristic of maturity.

College players are drafted for their skills. They're good, the best of the best. But their upside potential is also important. They're expected to get better, physically and mentally. They had what it took to get drafted, but will they take what they have and get better? If they do, they'll make the team, contribute to its success, and enjoy the benefits of an NFL career. If they don't, they'll be remembered as busts, if they're remembered at all.

Urlacher signed his contract early. He attended all the minicamps. He was in training camp from day one. By the third game he was a starter. And by the end of the season he was Defensive Rookie of the Year and a Pro Bowl alternate. He'd come a long way.

Our self-centeredness is the one opponent we all have to defeat if we expect to reach our upside potential as husbands. Oh sure, we can stay in the game if we don't, but we'll never play at the championship level. Not even close.

Our self-centeredness will show up in different ways in different situations in our marriages. It may be obvious, as seen in overtly demanding spouses. Their insistence on having their way is easily recognized. More subtle and less easily recognized are the acquiescent, what-a-nice-person spouses. They rarely assert themselves. The illusion of peace is the easy way out for them. Controllers and pleasers—both types serve themselves instead of the relationship. "For his good," "For her good," "For the good of the relationship," they both say. But both are destructive to the championship aspirations of the team. Most of us are probably somewhere between those two end points. Or maybe we react one way in a certain situation and another in a different situation. Some spouses can be demanding in one scenario and acquiescent in another.

Many spouses serve themselves when they avoid bringing up conflict. They feel it but don't try to deal with it productively. This used to be one of my favorites. I'd suck it up, stuff legitimate feelings, and carry on. I'd convince myself I was doing what was best for the team. In fact, I was taking the easy way out and serving myself.

Others may treat conflict as an opportunity to protect themselves or strengthen their position. Although they may hurt their spouses and the relationship in the process, to them staying in control or not getting hurt is more important.

Some men invest virtually all of their emotional capital in work. They insist they are doing it to provide for their families. There is certainly some truth to that. Maybe a lot of truth. But work is also an excuse behind which we often hide. It can be an easy escape. Many husbands find the complexities and challenges of their professional lives less intimidating than those of their marriages.

Some women invest virtually all of their emotional capital in their children. Being a parent is a consuming, 24/7 role. The love of a parent for a child is a powerful force, a mystery along the lines of Christ and the church, a husband and a wife. Regardless of how much parents do for a child, they can always do more. And the stakes are high. But some women devote themselves so completely to the role of mother that they shortchange their role as wife. This hurts their husbands and can damage their marriages. They also affect the development of their children by not showing them what a truly successful marriage looks like.

Some men are emotionally lazy. We expect a consistently satisfying sexual relationship. Nothing wrong with that. That's healthy. But it's not a realistic possibility if we don't work to create the emotional connection. If we don't do the work, our desire will seem more like a demand.

Some of us choose to go outside of marriage to satisfy our sexual desires through affairs, fantasy, or pornography. It's the path of least resistance to easy pleasure. It's easier than the sometimes-tough work of understanding ourselves and our wives, which is required for emotional connection.

And some women are sexually lazy. Their God-given desire for deep emotional connection never goes away. It can't and it shouldn't. But they don't make sexual intimacy with their husband a priority. They allow themselves to be consumed by various interests and activities that distract them and absorb their time. Women may be as prone to emotional fantasies as men are to sexual fantasies. They take their own path of least resistance to the things that are most important to them. Their relationships suffer as a result.

Do any of these sound like your marriage? Maybe. Maybe not. Inaccurate stereotypes, or a ring of truth? Every marriage is different.

So are every husband and every wife. What's consistent is that each of us wants to have relationships in ways that are easiest for us. Identifying what that looks like in our own marriage is the different part.

Self-centeredness isn't confined exclusively to the ways husbands and wives directly relate to each other. The way we conduct our thoughts, activities, and relationships when we're on our own will go a long way toward determining whether or not we win the marriage game.

It's been said that character is who you are when nobody's looking. That's certainly true in marriage. And nobody's looking at our thoughts, so we have to ask ourselves a couple of questions about our thoughts. Are we laying the solid foundation necessary for honest connection? Or are we creating a weak foundation, built with deception and selfishness? That weak foundation invariably results in an unstable, ineffective team.

Rookie spouses make rookie mistakes. I know I did. Early in our marriage things weren't going as I expected. The work was harder than I had anticipated. The positive feelings associated with building a powerful, mature love weren't as frequent or intense as those that had accompanied falling in love. I felt frustrated and disappointed but didn't know why. It had to be somebody's fault, most likely Tari's. At least that's what I sometimes felt. In reality, it was my own discomfort at having my weaknesses exposed and my expectations unmet that frustrated me. There wasn't an *I* in *team* at that point in my marriage.

But I hung with it. I tried to understand Tari's needs better and tried to put them ahead of my own. I tried to put into practice the idea of serving one another in love. I started to think I was improving as a husband. And I'm sure I was improving. To succeed as a husband involves making sacrifices. I knew I was making sacrifices as a husband in order to grow in my role and to serve Tari. I was experiencing a certain amount of success.

An unfortunate by-product of success is that it often arouses our sense of entitlement. Entitlement is the most tenacious part of this tendency to think first of ourselves. Sometimes the more successful we are in an endeavor, the more entitled we feel. Like everyone else, I've been conditioned to believe that sacrifices should equal rewards. Though I wish I could tell you that the rewards I feel entitled to are always noble and long-term, the truth is that I'm more often focused on pleasurable and short-term.

As a husband, I've sometimes wondered what I'm entitled to as a result of the sacrifices I'm making. *What does my success entitle me to? What's in it for me? If I do this, what do I get out of it?*

Sound Christlike to you? Me neither. And after twelve years of marriage, how often do I play against my self-centeredness? Every day. The game is never over. An NFL team must play each Sunday; last week doesn't matter. And yesterday doesn't matter to me as a husband. Every day I know I'll be lining up against my inclination to think of myself. Winning is an ongoing process, not a conclusive event.

Is my wife prone to self-centeredness? Certainly.

Does she need to grow? Yes.

Can I do that for her? No.

Will I have to address the challenges that her self-centeredness brings to the marriage? No question.

But I can't defeat her self-centeredness for her any more than she can defeat mine for me. It is inefficient and destructive to the team for either of us to try. But if I beat mine, she's in a much better position to beat hers. It's all about the direction of the relationship and the momentum we create.

Once a newlywed makes the transition from rookie husband to experienced veteran, the marriage game slows down. He understands marriage and his wife a little better. He's more confident. He knows he has what it takes to succeed. There's danger there, as well. Knowing you've got what it takes to succeed is not the same as doing it.

Life can become so numbingly routine that we fail to respect our opponent. Our self-centeredness beats us on a play or two. No big deal. Then we drop a game. Okay, it won't happen again. Before we recognize what is going on, we may have spent years battling the wrong opponent. Our self-centeredness came up with a different game plan, a new way to get us to focus on ourselves instead of our wives. We failed to adapt, so the losses started piling up.

Yes, it's a different level of competition in marriage, and many spouses never make the adjustment. The learning curve for a rookie is as steep in marriage as it is in the NFL.

One good play in a good game. One good game in a good season. One good season in…the story of Brian Urlacher's career is still being written.

"I think I made more mistakes than I did tackles," was Urlacher's modest assessment of his first start. "There were a few plays where I wasn't in my gap. I have to change that. I've got a lot to learn."

He does have a lot to learn. He developed fast for a rookie, but he has a long way to go. Shedding blockers and getting to the ball-carrier is all part of the game. There is as much upside potential as downside risk, but the Bears will never have to worry about Urlacher's ability to recognize his opponent.

Husbands and wives should be so lucky.

The Extra Point

It's the game everyone wants to see. John Madden and Al Michaels in the booth, sixty thousand people in the stands, and a national audience in front of their televisions. It's showtime for *Monday Night Football*. The world is going to see what you've got. You want to play your best. Instead, Madden has you on the replay.

"Right here. See how he feels the conflict. He's disappointed, probably angry, maybe even hurt. But he doesn't talk about it. He avoids it, stuffs it, takes the easy way out. Boom! You see how self-centeredness rides him right out of the play. If they're going to have a shot at winning this marriage game, he's going to have to figure out how to handle conflict instead of conflict handling him."

Later in the half.

"Look here. Remember how her day went at work. Tough day. She needs her teammate to listen, just listen. That's what he's supposed to do on this play. But he's had a tough day too. See how distracted he is. He's working on the computer at home. Grunts a couple of replies. See, he never stops, never engages, never works up the energy to pay attention. Easy way out. Boom! His self-centeredness drops her right there."

———

If the opponent you line up against every day is self-centeredness, your desire to have marriage in ways that are easiest for you, how would you rate your competitiveness?

Compared to your rookie season in marriage, in what areas have you made the most progress?

In what ways does your self-centeredness still affect your relationship?

A Fool for a Coach

*A good coach will make his players see what they can
become rather than what they are.*

—Ara Parseghian

The creative Bill Walsh has but three, which is one more
than his Super Bowl XIX counterpart, the NFL's win-
ningest head coach, Don Shula, has. If the heavily favored Baltimore
Colts had beaten the Jets in Super Bowl III, Chuck Noll would have
five. Instead, Joe Namath came through on his guaranteed victory,
and Noll has "only" four.

Buddy Ryan has two, as does Bill Arnsparger, and Lynn Stiles
has three. They are three of the four coaches who have the distinc-
tion of going to Super Bowls with a record three different teams.
Dan Reeves is the fourth and, although his nine Super Bowl appearances as a coach are more than anyone else's, he only has two rings to
show for it.

A Super Bowl win and the ring that goes with it are precious.
Only seventeen teams know what a Super Bowl victory is like. Just

ten have won more than once. A Super Bowl ring is the picture that is worth a thousand words. It represents innumerable hours devoted to the craft of football.

"You can go to the bank and borrow money," explained former Steelers' tackle Joe Greene, "but you can't go to the bank and borrow a Super Bowl ring." He should know. He earned four as a player.

One for the thumb? It is a very select group of coaches who have five Super Bowl rings. A coach has to be associated with excellent football teams. Seven of the NFL's thirty-two teams have never been to the Super Bowl. Another eight have been only once.

The team with the most appearances? Dallas. The Cowboys have played in eight Super Bowls and are tied for the most victories with five. No Dallas coach has five Super Bowl rings, though. Denver has the second highest number of Super Bowl appearances—six. Unfortunately, they are also tied with Buffalo and Minnesota for the most losses—four.

"He's forgotten more football than I know," said Mike Shanahan, a man who knows football well enough to have three rings of his own, as he described one of the members of the 5-5-1 club—the five coaches who earned five Super Bowl rings with one team.

Though he coached in one of the NFL's most visible and successful programs, his anonymity was assured. He was not one of the guys prowling the sideline in headphones who huddled with the quarterback during time-outs. Nor was he one of the coordinators in the press box overseeing the game while calling plays and adjustments down to the coaches on the field.

"The very basis of coaching is the knowledge you possess and how well it is imparted," the Hall of Fame head coach said. "The bottom line is: Did the athletes under your direction reach their full potential?"

Eleven of his players were named All Pro, though you could never tell by their statistics. As a group they totaled only three receptions, one for a touchdown and two kickoff returns for 13 yards. He coached the men that statistics forgot. Their individual careers are measured by years of service and games played.

Their team effectiveness, however, is more quantifiable. His men learned their skills so well and executed them so effectively that the league's first 1,000-1,000 man rushed and received his way to 2,066 total yards in 1985. They held defenders at bay long enough for the two most efficient quarterbacks ever to toss a spiral to scan the field, often finding the league's all-time leading receiver and scorer in the process.

If it's head coaches who get the credit or blame, it's the position coaches who get the job done. They are the ones who work hands on with the players to develop their individual skill sets and to blend those individual skills into the needs of the team. People talk of the "skill positions"—quarterbacks, receivers, running backs, and maybe defensive backs. The implication is that all the rest are just running around colliding with each other.

When the assistant was asked by his head coach to develop a list of the skills and fundamentals required for success at the position he coached, he came up with thirty. It was a sweet science of reverse shoulder blocks, cut blocks, and misdirection that he taught. Forsaking the prevailing bigger-is-better trend toward size, he placed a premium on quickness and functional intelligence. He prized skill and technique, and it worked.

"[He] has developed more offensive line knowledge than anyone, ever," said the head coach. "I learned more about football from him in one day than I knew when I first set foot at 4949 Centennial Boulevard. I felt his energy, his passion every day. He's the best coach I've ever been around," claimed Jon Gruden, one of the men with whom he shared assistant coaching duties.

He watched without envy as peers like Shanahan and Gruden—as well as Mike Holmgren, Brian Billick, Dennis Green, and many others—went on to become successful NFL head coaches. He chose to remain a position coach. "I'd rather teach than be an administrator," he said.

The fact that he was such an effective teacher should have come as no surprise. He was valedictorian of his high school class and an honors student as an undergraduate at Oregon State University, where he also earned a Master's of Education degree. The fact that he chose a tough classroom like the NFL in which to teach is no surprise, either. He was an officer in the marines.

"[He] is the spirit of the [team]," said the man who brought him on board in 1979. "He is the single person who has been with the club through five world championships and a dynasty, and he's played a major role in building that dynasty. Without [him], we wouldn't have those Super Bowl trophies."

"I found out a long time ago that the players are the game" is the way the coach summarized his coaching philosophy. "It's about being able to work together for the same goal. That's more important than me getting my way or them getting their way."

And in working together toward the same goal, they achieved an unequaled level of success. Only one team with more than one Super Bowl win is undefeated in the NFL's showcase game. The San Francisco 49ers are the league's elite with a 5-0 record—five wins in fourteen seasons and five rings for five coaches who were there the whole time.

"If anybody around here goes to the Hall of Fame as a coach, I think he should," said Pete Carroll, a man with whom he shared assistant duties before moving on to take head coaching positions, first at New England then at USC. "He's the guy who's lived through it all and kept it going.... He's been the guy. He's an icon."

The team was built on the offense. The offense was built on the line. "Check out the Super Bowl winners down through the years: some had a great running game, others had great receivers. *All* had a great line," claims Joe Montana.

The 49ers line was built on one man, the late Bobb McKittrick. He understood the goal, how to fit his men into the accomplishment of that goal, how to teach them what they had to do, and how to get the most out of them.

A COACH IN THE MARRIAGE GAME

"He's the most teachable guy I've ever had. He reflects on what we talk about. He's a good listener. He asks clarifying questions. He applies the things we talk about." That's not McKittrick recalling any of his linemen; that's Rick Mink, the man who for years headed up the marriage ministry at Willow Creek Community Church, talking about Kevin, a three-year veteran of the marriage game.

Kevin understood the player-coach relationship. As a high school wrestler, he had learned the value of a coach. A coach sees things the athlete doesn't and is more experienced. A coach will help an athlete get better. But first the athlete has to want to improve. Second, the coach has to know what he's talking about. And third, a trust relationship between the player and coach must be established.

The desire to learn and grow carried over to Kevin's adult professional life. He wanted to get better, so he attended seminars, read books, and listened to tapes. Whether the arena was athletics or business, he understood the value of obtaining different perspectives in order to grow. So when he entered his church's marriage preparation process, it was with an open mind and desire to learn.

Kevin's parents had always been very supportive and encouraging of his academic studies, his athletic pursuits, and his career. He describes them as loving, gracious people. They immediately welcomed Nadia, Kevin's wife, to the family and made her feel every bit as loved as their son. Kevin is grateful to his parents for all they have done for him and taught him.

However, Kevin did not learn from them the skill set necessary to have a Super Bowl marriage. His parents are still together, but like many of us, he knew he wanted to do his marriage differently.

Nor did he learn a skill set for a successful marriage in his dating life. He describes his premarital days as "serial monogamy"—a series of relationships he consistently broke off once things started to get serious. Like many men, he entered marriage having never experienced a successful long-term relationship with a woman.

Kevin and Nadia wanted input from Rick and his wife, JoAn, their mentors in the marriage-prep process. The difference between growth and stagnation, between a marriage that is achieving its potential and one that is falling short, is the quality of information people receive and how they respond to it.

Kevin is what every coach hopes for in a player: he not only takes in the information, but he is willing to make changes in order to improve. When Rick and JoAn pointed out that premarital sex is inconsistent with a biblical approach to dating, Kevin and Nadia investigated that claim. They came to the conclusion that Rick and JoAn were right, so they committed to sexual purity.

Rick and JoAn said that living together before marriage is inconsistent with the Bible and that, according to many studies, it is a hindrance to the success of the marriage. Kevin and Nadia looked into it for themselves, and Kevin moved in with his brother-in-law. Knowledge is one thing, execution another.

Those clearly countercultural choices were not easy, but once Kevin and Nadia became convinced of their biblical validity, they opted for the road less traveled—much less traveled these days. A good coach will stretch you.

Rick wanted Kevin to have a one-on-one opportunity to meet with him if Kevin wanted to pursue it, so Rick invited him to lunch. Their relationship stretches over two years now, and they still meet once a month. One reason is that Kevin doesn't simply make the changes and hope for the best. He continues to interact with Rick on how the new approaches are succeeding and always strives to get better.

Kevin's willingness to learn isn't confined solely to his relationship with Rick. Two different church services taught him a critical lesson in the skill of listening. He learned that a person who is experiencing something on an emotional level does not necessarily want a solution. He discovered there is often more value in being available and in listening than in trying to fix the problem or offering something profound.

Those lessons were invaluable when Nadia's sister passed away. It's the kind of stress that exposes the weaknesses of a marriage—and its strengths. Kevin suddenly found himself in the unfamiliar role of being a comforter. It's a role that many of us are not normally comfortable with. Unless we have been coached to do otherwise, most of us return to what comes naturally in stressful situations. Kevin responded by listening, which is what Nadia really needed.

He has set a goal to read one marriage-related book a year, and Kevin and Nadia try to attend one retreat or seminar annually to work on their marriage. That's important. Not every church has an effective premarital process, if they have one at all. And not every spouse has a mentor he or she can meet with in order to grow. However, books and seminars, magazines like *Marriage Partnership,* and Web sites like growthtrac.com can provide valuable insights. They're also easy to access.

Kevin also has written goals for specific areas in his marriage in which he wants to improve. His life isn't standing still. His marriage isn't standing still. And he knows that he can't stand still as a husband. But in spite of his willingness to learn and his determination to improve, he still drops the ball. Regardless of the quality of the coaching and the skill of the husband, mistakes will be made in any marriage. The game is never over when you're lining up against self-centeredness and you're playing on the road.

"I still fail every day at marriage," Kevin admits, "and I still need to pick myself up every day and try to do better the next." The old coaching saying "We're not where we want to be. We're not where we ought to be. But thank goodness we're not where we used to be!" could certainly apply to Kevin.

One of the areas he is working on is listening more and reacting less. He admits that he is sometimes defensive when Nadia brings up an opportunity for growth in the way he relates to her. Some things are easier to hear from Rick than from Nadia. Rick has a more experienced perspective. He's also more objective and can focus on what's right for the relationship rather than what's easy for Kevin. He knows the goal they are shooting for, and he has their best interests at heart. Because of the time they have invested in their relationship, Rick has earned Kevin's complete trust. Competence and trust are the foundation of the player-coach relationship.

Coaches are not always beloved by the players they coach against. Howie Long was once so enraged by the tactics of the 49ers linemen that he charged after McKittrick following the game. Tim Green, formerly with the Atlanta Falcons, recalls that 49er linemen would "hook you, grab you, pull you, punch you, kick you, leg-whip you, or dive at the back of your knees in their effort to keep you out of a play." That's why Green called McKittrick "Dr. Mean." But Green also expressed respect for him and the effectiveness of his players. It was about results.

The marriage game is also about results. Are we becoming better husbands? We probably aren't able to answer that for ourselves; we need the input of others. A good coach will tell us things we might not want to hear. He'll help us see what we need to do to improve. And he'll challenge us to reach the next level. But don't expect it to be easy. A Super Bowl win isn't easy for an NFL team, and neither is a Super Bowl marriage for a couple.

It's important to seek input on our marriages and then act on that input. Spouses who do are on their way to utilizing perhaps the single most important resource they have for developing as a partner: their own mates. "Men who let their wives influence them have happier marriages and are less likely to divorce than men who resist their wives' influence," say marriage researchers John Gottman and Nan Silver. Accepting a wife's influence and acting on that input is a learned skill, however. It takes practice. Unfortunately, many of us are more invested in personal victories than team victories. We're more interested in feeling like we're right than in getting better. We're often more interested in what it takes to get by rather than what it takes to move the team ahead.

"Research shows that a husband who can accept influence from his wife also tends to be an outstanding father. He is relationally more skilled, better able to connect with his wife and his children." He is most likely better able to connect with himself, as well. And that's a critical skill in the process of becoming a better spouse.

As our relationship skill set improves, we'll improve as husbands and fathers. But we'll also become a coach for our wives. Women *may* be more relationally skilled than men, but they still need help. Our thoughts, feelings, needs, and expectations can be as mysterious to our wives as theirs are to us.

Gottman and Silver also report that women are more likely to accept influence from their husbands. It may be gender predisposition or social training or both. And though it is a good trait to have, wives need to make sure they continue to learn, stay receptive to influence, and grow throughout their marriages.

NFL coaches need to master the knowledge necessary for their players to succeed. Just as important, they need to be able to impart that information to the players in ways they understand. Finally, they need to monitor the results, offering encouragement and feedback so that the players are in an upward spiral of improvement. Super Bowl coaches do that; so do Super Bowl husbands.

A husband needs to develop expertise in the area of his own

needs and expectations. He has to have knowledge of the things that are important to him. Then he has to communicate those to his wife in ways she can understand and will respond to positively.

The humility to learn and the loving patience to teach—these traits don't come easily to many men in the context of marriage. Exercising influence takes as much work as receiving it. Unfortunately, many of us only begin to understand what our needs and expectations are when they are not met. That can result in frustration and disappointment. We can sometimes express important and relevant information as demands, accusations, or judgments. And these can be tough for our wives to receive. Before a man can become a coach for his wife, he may need to improve in conflict management. That's not necessarily easy. But a husband who is focused on the goal of a Super Bowl marriage will pay the price to achieve it.

If our wives are not meeting our needs, we need to ask ourselves why. Do our wives know what our needs are? Have we created an environment of security, respect, and trust, an environment in which they feel safe? Have we done our job as marriage teammates so they are free to be the wives we want them to be? A husband can't do a wife's job, but neither can she if she doesn't know how or doesn't feel safe trying. In order to reach the Super Bowl, a player needs an environment where instruction is given and failure is accepted as part of the process of improvement. So do husbands and wives.

A good coach—whether it's a mentor or a partner—will help a husband see what his relationship tendencies are, both good and bad. The coach can reinforce the good ones in the husband and challenge him on the bad ones. The coach will help him discern who his opponent really is and how he is operating. The coach will help him understand how a couple's different personalities can result in frustrating dynamics if they don't learn how to honor and accept their differences. The coach can help him see how sloppy execution leads to predictably disappointing results. And a good coach can help a husband understand how past relationships have shaped his attitudes and skills and what role they are playing in his marriage.

An awareness of past relationship patterns is especially important in determining the influence of the families we grew up in. We think of ourselves as discerning, objective adults who make thoughtful, properly motivated decisions. But we may be more affected by our families than we realize. Our earliest lessons about ourselves and how spouses relate to each other were taught to us by our parents. And those lessons, whether helpful or not, come together powerfully in our own marriages, though we probably won't recognize them. To us they are normal. To us they are just the way relationships are conducted.

"We either overcompensate for what we didn't get from our own parents," warns Dr. Harville Hendrix, "or blindly re-create the same painful situations." That's a statement with profound implications for our marriages. A coach can help us understand how true it is for us.

When a man reads a book on marriage, he shows his general commitment to his marriage team. When he solicits the input of another man, he shows a commitment to improving. When he asks his wife, "How am I doing as a husband?" he shows the humility necessary to learn. When he takes information from all of these sources and grows as a result, he shows his passion for winning.

"The athlete who coaches himself has a fool for a coach." Every coach knows that. So do the players. Kevin knows that marriage is simply too important to take a chance on what he thinks he knows about it. Losing a football game is one thing. Losing in the marriage game is another.

Winning a Super Bowl ring is a tremendous accomplishment for both the players and the coaches who teach them. But winning a Super Bowl ring in marriage—now that's an accomplishment!

The Extra Point

Size. Balance. Quick feet. Strength. You were blessed from the start. You combined a tenacious work ethic with a competitive fire to develop as one of the nation's top high school linemen. You could have gone anywhere to college but chose USC because you felt you had a good shot at a national championship, and the Trojans' passing emphasis would help you develop into an NFL-quality lineman.

It worked. First-round draft choice. Certain to get a good look and compete for a starting position. It's all upside, except you start getting beat in the minicamps. It goes from bad to worse as the defensive linemen run over and around you, consistently getting to the quarterback. You miss your assignment on the runs as well.

You've always excelled at this game; now you're confused, and it shows. Your frustration mounts.

"Settle down," says the line coach as he pulls you aside. "Just think about what we've taught you. We know you're going to make mistakes; just don't make the same ones over and over. Now, let's start with that last play…" You trust him, so you listen. He knows what he is talking about.

———

Who is helping you become a better husband?

Can you and your wife be effective coaches for each other?

Playing Hurt

Football is a great game, and it will teach you an
awful lot.… It will build character, but it also
reveals character. You'll learn whether you can or
can't play, whether you can take that hard lick
and get back up or stay down.

—JOHNNY UNITAS

hen [he] didn't get up, I knew it was bad," said the guard. In the four years since the running back had left the University of Florida following his junior season, the guard had been opening holes for him. "It takes an awful lot to keep him on the ground."

It was the final game of the season. Both teams were assured a spot in the playoffs, but the outcome of this contest had huge post-season implications. The victor would win the division outright, get a first-week bye, and secure home-field advantage throughout the playoffs. Theirs was a division you wanted to win. It had produced the last three Super Bowl champions. The loser would be relegated to the uncertainties of the wild-card round.

The back had proven his value immediately at every level of competition. He was a schoolboy wonder at Florida's Escambia High. He rushed for 115 yards and two touchdowns in his first start as a freshman. He had led the team to consecutive state championships, totaling nearly 9,000 yards by the time he graduated four years later.

It took him all of three games to crack the University of Florida's starting lineup as a freshman. In that game, he carried thirty-nine times for a school-record 224 yards and scored two touchdowns in a 23–14 upset of Alabama in Tuscaloosa. Three years and 3,704 yards later, he joined the first college underclass to declare eligibility for the NFL draft.

"I think we got a _____ of a back," said the coach after taking him with the seventeenth pick of the draft, "but we'll have to get another in five years. This one's going to burn out pretty quick." The coach was justifiably concerned that weekly NFL-style poundings would quickly reduce the effectiveness of the five-foot-nine, 209-pound runner.

The new level of competition was nothing more than another arena in which he could prove his value. As a rookie he was fifth in the NFC in rushing, coming within 63 yards of the 1,000-yard benchmark and earning Offensive Rookie of the Year honors. He ran for 1,563 yards the following season to lead the entire NFL. He trumped that the next year by again leading the league in rushing with 1,713 yards. His fifty-nine receptions were the most by any running back that year, and his nineteen touchdowns made him the league's top nonkicking scorer. In games in which the running back carried the ball twenty or more times, his team was 29-1; when he rushed for 100 or more yards, they were 22-1. He had been named to the Pro Bowl in each of his first three years and never missed a game.

Runner, receiver, scorer—an MVP in the making, the kind of guy you could count on. His coaches counted on him. His teammates counted on him.

When it came time for a new contract after his third season, the owner counted on him, too...to take less money than he was worth. The back had honored his original three-year contract and put up MVP numbers. Now he simply wanted to be paid commensurately. The back and the owner differed in their assessment of his worth, however—a difference of about $6 million over four years. Let the games begin.

Training camp came and went. No running back. Four preseason games came and went. No running back. "[He] is a luxury, not a necessity for [us]," insisted the team owner at one point in the negotiations.

The first regular-season game came and went, a 35–16 thrashing by the Redskins. No running back. The home opener came and went, a 13–10 loss to Buffalo. No running back. No team had ever started a season 0-2 and made it to the Super Bowl. The owner decided that perhaps he had misjudged the running back's importance to the team. The two sides quickly came to an agreement. The back was in uniform for the third game, in which he carried the ball a modest eight times for 45 yards.

He carried the team the rest of the season. His 1,486 yards earned him his third consecutive rushing title, only the fourth time that had ever happened. The offense that had sputtered in the first two weeks found itself and ended the season as the NFL's second-highest scoring unit. As they entered the final week of the season, the team's record stood at 11-4, 11-2 since the back's return.

They needed this game, and their strategy for winning it was simple—get him the ball. Hand it to him. Pass it to him. What the heck, why not sneak him onto the field on defense, too.

Near the end of the first half, he tore through an enormous hole off right tackle, juked a defensive back, and took off downfield. Forty-six yards later, a safety slammed him into the turf, separating his shoulder. Uh-oh, a little glitch in the game plan. He'd already touched the ball twenty-five times and piled up 151 yards in offense while leading his team to a 10–0 lead. They managed another field goal and headed into the locker room at the half nursing a 13–0 lead.

The trainers worked on his shoulder through the halftime break and even into the third quarter as the defense took the field after the kickoff. His two goals for the season had been to help his team win a Super Bowl title and to earn a rushing title for himself. His thoughts were on the rushing title as he emerged from the tunnel just in time to see his team's punt returner fumble away a punt. The defense surrendered a quick score, and suddenly their lead was less than a touchdown.

"From that moment on, I never even considered the rushing title," said the back. "I was just out there to win." The gap was closed to 13–10 at the end of the third quarter. Though still playing, he wasn't dominating as he had in the first half. Every hit he took lit him up with pain but none more than when he hit the frozen ground under a defender in the fourth quarter and heard a pop inside his chest.

"Are you okay?" asked his coach as he came to the sideline. "Do you wanna go? Just tell me if you can't, because we'll put Lincoln [his backup] in there."

"No way I was sitting down now," the back remembers. "I was into this thing too deep." The defense gave up another field goal to tie the game at 13 all, which is where it stood as time expired. Overtime.

After their defense held, the back and the rest of the offense headed back out for their first overtime possession. The back figured he'd be used as a decoy. He figured wrong. With the game and season on the line, he got the ball on nine of his team's eleven plays in the overtime, gaining 41 yards on the drive and moving the team into field-goal position. The 41-yard field-goal attempt was good, giving the Dallas Cowboys a 16–13 win, the division championship, and a much-needed bye the following week.

"In my mind, this is still my best game," says career-rushing leader Emmitt Smith. "I had to dig deep…deeper than I thought I could go." And farther than he thought he could go. Smith rushed for 168 yards on thirty-two carries and caught ten passes for another 61 yards. A go-to guy? The Cowboys ran seventy plays. The ball was in Smith's hands on forty-two of them. He accounted for 229 of Dallas's 339 total yards. Seventy-eight of those yards, a good day's work for most backs, came after the injury.

The 1993 Dallas Cowboys became the first team to start a season 0-2 and then go on to win the Super Bowl. The "luxury" they couldn't afford had become the necessity they couldn't live without. Emmitt Smith became the first back to defend his rushing title in spite of missing two games. He was named Offensive Player of the Year and league MVP.

"Football is not for the weak of mind or heart," says Smith. "You either put it on the line or you take up another sport."

Playing Through the Pain in Marriage

Putting yourself on the line is part of the deal in marriage, too. You probably already know this, but you're going to take some hits. There will be pain along the way. And some of the most painful hits will come from your wife. And some of the toughest hits she'll take will come from you. These are facts of married life. It shouldn't be that way, but it is. Our ability to play through pain in marriage will help determine what kind of marriage we have.

Don't get me wrong, a successful marriage is not a last-person-standing kind of thing. Husbands and wives are not supposed to hurt each other. And we're not called to silently endure hurtful, unloving, or disrespectful behavior. But we should expect a certain amount of it. We are imperfect people. Two imperfect people coming together are certain to cause each other some disappointment and frustration. We will know pain.

It's probably helpful to distinguish between pain and discomfort. Pain means something bad is happening. Pain is a hit we've taken from our spouses. We've been nailed by the marriage equivalent of a brutal block or tackle. Perhaps an injury has occurred. It's going to take a special effort to overcome the pain. And we may risk additional injury by doing so. Healing must occur.

Discomfort is different. There will be a certain amount of discomfort in any exertion. And the discomfort may mean that something positive is happening. Players lift weights, run sprints, and do drills to become stronger, faster, and more effective. They endure the discomfort in order to attain the benefits. They get better when they overcome discomfort.

The discomfort we feel in marriage could just be our old selves being transformed. It's bound to happen as we pursue a more Christlike character, but we go through the discomfort to attain the benefits. Marriage just happens to be where the transformation is taking place.

Much of what we think of as pain in marriage is really discomfort. But there will be pain in your marriage too. There will be times when you need a word of encouragement from your wife. Instead, you'll be blindsided by a sarcastic roll of the eyes. Will you obey your pain and do something to retaliate? Or will you take the hit and risk an additional one by staying engaged? There will be times when you go the extra mile in serving your wife, and she doesn't acknowledge or even notice it. Will you obey the pain you feel and do no more until she gives back? Or will you choose to obey your team's overarching 1 Corinthians 13, Galatians 5:13 approach and continue to serve in love?

There may be times in marriage when you will respectfully attempt to resolve conflict. Far from the calm discussion you expected, you might be met head-on with an emotional, hurtful comment. Will you obey the pain and withdraw from the relationship? Or will you remain calm and try again? There will be times when you will attempt to initiate sexual intimacy. Instead of the acceptance you'd hoped for, you might be drilled by distracted indifference that will feel like rejection. Will you obey your pain and withhold the emotional connection your wife needs and maybe start building a case for satisfying your desires in some other way? Or will you stay in the game and tell her why you're hurt?

These things and more will happen. And they won't just happen to you. You'll do them to your wife too. You may blindside her with a hurtful comment or sarcastic gesture. You may be the one who doesn't notice the things she does for you. Distracted indifference comes as easily to men as it does to women. With our busy lives and the numerous demands on our time and energy, we can overlook the needs of our wives. Not intentionally, you understand. There's just a lot going on.

You'll both wonder, *I thought we were playing on the same team.* You are! It's your self-centeredness that you're lining up against. When given a choice between the easy way out or the challenging way in, that easy way can look pretty appealing. Our natural inclination is to serve ourselves, not our partners. When we give, we're tempted to measure what we get in return.

We're all imperfect. A certain amount of disappointment, frustration, and hurt is bound to happen. And our self-interest is always hanging around. It's either hammering away at us to take the easy way or laying low, just waiting to be provoked. When hurt, we want to hurt back. When our mates disappoint us, we feel entitled to disappoint them. These little moments of truth will determine where your marriage is headed—toward the Christlike ideal or away from it.

What all of us have to decide is whether we will play with pain or sit this one out. Will we hang in there and continue to build the relationship, or will we withdraw? And here's something you should count on: you will face this choice time after time after time.

"In a league as violent as ours, a lot of people play hurt," Smith says. "I wanted to be a guy who could play hurt and still be effective." Nobody who plays regularly makes it through a season uninjured.

The little finger on the left hand of San Francisco defensive back Ronnie Lott was once crushed during the season. Given a choice between having the fingertip amputated or missing playoff games so it could heal, Lott chose amputation. He had to be there for his teammates.

Jim Otto has had thirty-eight major surgeries that stem from his time as the center for the Oakland Raiders. They include twenty-eight knee operations—*eight* of which were knee replacements—three back operations, and the replacement of both shoulders. His nose was broken so many times that he stopped counting at twenty. *Minor* injuries—things like broken fingers, a broken jaw, and concussions—are lumped together in a "various other" category. However, in a Hall of Fame career that lasted fifteen years, he never missed a regular-season game. Two hundred ten consecutive starts. Of course, he waited until after retiring for the replacement surgeries. As he said during his playing days, time off was for the off-season.

Not so for Donovan McNabb of the Philadelphia Eagles. McNabb missed six games of the 2002 season after suffering a broken leg in the first quarter of the tenth game. Yeah, he took a little time off. Not quite tough enough? Well, okay, he did finish the game in which he was hurt. And he did complete twenty of twenty-five passes for 255 yards and four touchdowns—after the injury. And he was back in time for the playoffs.

Playing through pain? Tell Jesus about it.

The pain was excruciating, but the outcome was still in doubt. People were depending on Him, so He continued. They had been through a lot in their three years together. It looked as if they had become a tight unit. Pressure situations can do that. But pressure can also tear a team apart.

In the end, Jesus's teammates scattered. When He most needed them, they weren't there. He knew it was going to happen, but that didn't make it any less painful.

It started with the beating.

"The soldier would use a whip of braided leather thongs with metal balls woven into them," begins Dr. Alexander Metherell's description of Jesus's crucifixion ordeal in Lee Strobel's book *The Case for Christ*. "When the whip would strike the flesh, these balls would cause deep bruises, or contusions, which would break open with further blows. And the whip had pieces of sharp bone as well, which would cut the flesh severely.

"The back would be so shredded that part of the spine was sometimes exposed by the deep, deep cuts. The whipping would have gone all the way from the shoulders down to the back, the buttocks, and the back of the legs."

Of course the beating was just the beginning. Jesus had not yet finished what He came to do, and neither had the soldiers.

"He would have been laid down, and his hands would have been nailed in the outstretched position to the horizontal beam.... The Romans used spikes that were five to seven inches long and tapered to a sharp point. They were driven through the wrist," Metherell continued. "This was a solid position that would lock the hand."

In the process, nerves in both hands would be crushed. The resulting pain defied description, so a new word was invented to convey the agony: *excruciating.* Once his hands were nailed to the crossbar, the cross would have been raised, certainly separating his shoulders. His feet were nailed to the cross as well, and the process of death by asphyxiation would begin.

"The reason is that the stresses on the muscles and diaphragm put the chest into the inhaled position; basically, in order to exhale, the individual must push up on his feet so the tension on the muscles would be eased for a moment....

"After managing to exhale, the person would then be able to relax down and take another breath in. Again he'd have to push himself up to exhale, scraping his bloodied back against the coarse wood of the cross. This would go on and on until complete exhaustion would take over." Unable to breathe any longer, the person would then die. If you saw *The Passion of the Christ,* you don't have to imagine this process.

"Father forgive them. They don't know what they're doing." At the end of it all, bearing the agony of crucifixion and the despair of absolute isolation, He still had the heart to pray for the people who were killing Him (see Luke 23:34).

Jesus had made His choices. Now He was experiencing the consequences. At the Last Supper, He could have despaired over how this was going to play out. He could have berated His disciples over the betrayal and abandonment that He knew was coming. Instead, He washed their feet, continued to teach, and went to pray. He could have obeyed the spirit of reluctance He must have felt in

Gethsemane, but He didn't. He prayed, then rose resolutely to meet His captors. When Pilate addressed Him after His beating, He could have obeyed the spirit of pain and pleaded for His release. That was not what He was committed to carrying out, however. Without regard to personal consequences, He honored that commitment.

His game hadn't quite ended. In spite of pain we can't even imagine, He couldn't give up. There was simply too much at stake. People's lives hung in the balance.

"It is finished," Jesus finally said. The price had been paid, but the story wasn't over. The whole story is not Jesus's willingness to humble Himself, to love, to serve, and even to die. It is His ability to do all those things and then to live again. That's what we should be paying attention to. He died, then rose.

"Love one another the way I loved you. This is the very best way to love. Put your life on the line for your friends" (John 15:12–13, MSG). *Okay,* we wonder, *maybe it is the very best way to love, but what's in it for me?*

We hear a lot about dying to self. Sometimes we get so wrapped up in the idea that we forget the point is not dying. The point is dying to our self-centeredness to be more effective in our relationships. We give up having relationships one way in order to have them in a better way. By giving out we are filled up.

"If you grasp and cling to life on your terms, you'll lose it," Jesus warns, "but if you let that life go, you'll get life on God's terms" (Luke 17:33, MSG). It's what we were made for. And it's what we're called to. Sure it's scary. It wouldn't be faith if it wasn't. But it's not as if Jesus is asking us to do something He didn't do.

The rewards of power, the comforts of entitlement, the respect of others, His very life—Jesus gave it all up, literally. He had nothing left. He accomplished what He set out to do. He told us to love. He told us how to love. Most important, He inspired us with history's greatest example of love. He put us in a position to succeed. He did His job; that's what great teammates do. When a teammate does his job, it frees us up to do ours.

Both husbands and wives have legitimate needs. And both husbands and wives are called to serve one another in love. So who goes first? As spouses, how much should we give? And if our mates don't respond as we'd hoped, should we continue to give? Who risks a hit? And if we take a hit, what then?

Ephesians 5:25 tells us to love our wives as Christ loved the church. You mean the Christ who left behind perfect community with the Father and the Spirit to become a man? You mean the Christ who participated in the creation of the world but relentlessly pursued individual relationships with people? You mean the Christ who never concerned Himself with what He was entitled to while He lived among men as an itinerant teacher? You mean the Christ who was still reaching out to people even as He was dying? You mean the Christ who, after rising from the dead, sought out those who had abandoned Him in order to restore the relationship?

That's our standard for our marriages? Yes.

Christ went first. He initiated the relationship with us. He took the hit. And He got back up. In spite of our failures, He continues to reach out.

Marriage is not for the weak of mind or heart. As Emmitt Smith said, "You either put it on the line or you take up another sport."

Jesus's willingness to take the hit, even to the point of death, is inspiring. However, His ability to die, then rise and love again is empowering. His life gives men an example to *see* and the power to *do.*

The Extra Point

Your teammate heads for the sideline to stop the clock. First-and-ten from their 26, 1:30 left, and you're down by two.

A field goal wins it, you think as the play winds down, and you start to slow up. *But from here, no sure thing. Another first down would...*

Pow! Helmet to ear hole. You're down, stunned for a moment until your competitive instincts take over. You can't let whoever just blindsided you get away with it. It's a matter of pride, so you jump up and take a swing.

Here comes the flag. Sure it was a cheap shot, but it's always the second guy who gets caught. Justified or not, you just cost your team 15 yards and moved it out of field-goal range. You took your eyes off the bigger goal and responded instinctively to the pain, and it may cost your team the game.

Would you say your big picture of marriage is clear and strong enough to enable you to endure the discomfort of overcoming your self-centeredness?

When your spouse—either deliberately or accidentally, through action or inaction—hurts you, do you stay focused on the goal, continue to pursue connection, and risk another hit? Or do you shut down or lash out?

The Will to Prepare

[Mike Shanahan] taught me to believe that through prepa-
ration—not just by a casual glance at your work or even
solid preparation, but by a deep, penetrating preparation—
you are going to be tough to beat. He taught me how to be
a better player by not relying on my athletic ability and
natural talents…but also on hard work.

—STEVE YOUNG

It was January 1986. A college reunion of sorts, although maybe
a little more physical than the usual "Hey, do you remember
the time…" affairs you and I go to.

The eyes of Texas had been upon them when they had gotten
together in 1979 and 1980. The linebacker was in his junior and
senior years of an all-American collegiate career at Baylor. The halfback was in his freshman and sophomore years at SMU. The linebacker hit so forcefully that he cracked sixteen of his own helmets in
college. He pursued ball-carriers so relentlessly that he averaged fifteen tackles per game, including games against Alabama, Ohio State,

and Arkansas in which he made thirty, thirty-one, and thirty-three tackles respectively. His play was so consistent that he was twice honored as the Southwest Conference Player of the Year. He was a consensus all-American two times.

So why did he last until the second round of the NFL draft in the spring of '81? At an even six feet tall and 220 pounds, he raised understandable concern about his ability to survive as a middle linebacker in the pros. But his zeal and knack for being in the right place at the right time more than made up for his lack of size. And by the eighth game he was a starter.

That same year the junior halfback was a second-team all-American. In 1982, his senior season, he rushed for 1,617 yards and finished third in the Heisman Trophy balloting while also earning consensus all-American honors. At six foot three, 230 pounds, his size raised no concerns. He was the second player taken in the '83 draft, right after the Baltimore Colts had picked John Elway.

Both had breakout NFL seasons in 1983. The linebacker was named to the NFC squad for the Pro Bowl, the first of ten consecutive times he would earn that honor. The halfback immediately became the featured back in the offense. He rushed for a league-high 1,808 yards, still a rookie record, and was named All Pro. He averaged 5.6 yards a carry on his way to a single-season record of 2,105 yards the following season. The promise each had shown in college was coming to fruition in the pros.

As their personal stars rose, so did the fortunes of their respective teams. Both teams won their division in 1985.

A player doesn't get to the NFL without preparation. Hundreds of high school and college practices, innumerable hours watching game film, thousands of reps in the weightroom, countless wind sprints—all these things put athletes in the position to be drafted by a NFL team, where it starts all over again.

The key to NFL success is preparation, both physical and mental. Well-prepared players arrive at training camp in shape. They know what they have to do to contribute to the team. They are in good enough physical condition to overcome fatigue, injuries, and opponents so they can make that contribution.

Thorough preparation is a prerequisite to effective performance. Natural ability can take a player a long way, but the further he goes, the tougher the competition. All players have the physical skills in the NFL. The difference often lies in preparation. Games can be won or lost by the tiniest increments of performance. And those tiny increments will be determined by how well prepared a player is.

The linebacker's preparation was legendary. He knew he couldn't wait until July training camp to get ready for the regular assortment of NFC Central Division rivals and the other foes the league schedule makers would throw his way. If he waited to get ready, he wouldn't be ready. Every morning in the off-season he went to the hill, about 60 yards from top to bottom, to prepare for his opponents. Up the hill he ran, ten times forward and ten times backward. Up the hill he ran sideways, ten times leading with his right side, ten with his left. His afternoon sessions at the track were a torturous mix of sprints: 110s, 220s, and 330s, with 880s thrown in for variety.

His preparation didn't stop with off-season conditioning. During the season he was a fanatical student of game films. He began his study of the upcoming opponent on Sunday night. He would pick up films on his way home after that day's game. By the time the coaches began reviewing film with the rest of the team on Wednesday, the linebacker had already spent hours searching for clues to a team's situational tendencies. Down and distance, formation and personnel, even minute tip-offs an individual player might give by a slight change in his stance—the linebacker looked for anything he could leverage into a competitive advantage.

"When you see the linebacker get to the ball a step late, he takes as much punishment as the ball-carrier," he said in assessing his approach to the game. "He may have a lot to do with the tackle, but he's hit as much as he hits, takes as much as he gives, and it's not as much fun. The key to avoiding that is to get that repetition in your mind from the film all week. Then, when you see the play coming on the field, you have to convince yourself that you're right. Anticipate and get there."

The week before his reunion with his old adversary, the linebacker had done a lot of anticipating and getting there. He had led his defense to a 21–0 shutout of the Eastern Division champion, the New York Giants.

Nobody wants to show up at a reunion looking anything less than his best. The halfback was no exception. He had led his team to a rout of Dallas by rushing for a playoff-record 248 yards, including touchdown runs of 40 and 55 yards. Both players would be bringing their A games to the championship contest.

The two had gotten together a couple of times, in '83 and '84. The halfback's team had prevailed both times. Those were November games in sunny California, however. Not inconsequential, but not the playoffs, either. Now the running back's team was on the road, and if they were going to win, they would have to do what the Giants had been unable to do the week before: run the ball in cold, windy conditions.

In the first quarter the visitors faced a third-and-one, one foot that is. An average-sized man can fall and gain a foot, if he falls forward. A superbly conditioned six-foot-three man with a running start behind one of the NFL's largest offensive lines should be able to pound out a foot. It was a line of reasoning that made sense to their head coach. He chose to send his All Pro halfback into the line behind his left guard and tackle. Strength against strength, a little "Let's see what you got!"

At the snap of the ball, the guard stepped to his left.

"By that time I'd seen that play a hundred times," recalled the linebacker, referring to his film study. It was a simple play based on an X-block between the guard and tackle, a short-yardage staple of the offense. "When they ran that play, I just took off."

As soon as the guard stepped to kick out, the linebacker knew the tackle was coming to block down. He had prepared for this moment. He'd seen it on film. He knew where he would find his old college pal, so he headed for the hole between the guard and tackle. He knew what was coming, but he still had to make the tackle for no gain. He had to be right with conviction.

As the halfback headed for the line of scrimmage, he ran into his old college buddy, who wrapped him up in a familiar embrace and, with the help of his teammates, dropped him for a loss.

Though the score was only 10–0 late in the first quarter, the game was over. There would be no 200 yards rushing or long touchdown runs for Eric Dickerson, the former SMU Mustang, that day. The message sent by the linebacker and his teammates was simple: "We're a better football team. Your strength against ours, and you can't even gain a foot when you have to."

As the linebacker headed off the field, he erupted in the kind of spontaneous scream that earned him the nickname Samurai. It was a scream of enthusiasm, exhortation, and personal satisfaction. Mike Singletary, the undersized linebacker from Baylor, was prepared, as were the rest of the Chicago Bears. Two weeks later the Bears routed the New England Patriots in one of the most lopsided Super Bowls ever played.

PREPPING FOR THE MARRIAGE GAME

Once in a while when Tari and I were dating, we'd get into an argument over some little thing. It always seemed so out of proportion—little thing, big blowup. The blowups were sometimes in person, sometimes over the phone, but the result was always the same. Both of us would feel we had suffered some offense, and there was a coldness between us.

I'd always wonder, *What was that about?* It wasn't as though either of us was picking a fight. Usually it was a tone-of-voice thing. She'd say something in a way that would hit me wrong. And I'd say something in a tone of voice that would hit her wrong. Instead of stepping back and calming down, we'd escalate.

Eventually I became aware of a pattern. Within a couple of days of these incidents, I would learn Tari was having her period. Not surprisingly, the pattern continued once we married. I discovered two additional patterns. Tari has a very regular cycle. I can predict with great accuracy when she will most likely be discouraged, sensitive, sad, moody, upset, or argumentative. I have also discovered that the blowups are rarely of the stereotypical "irrational, nagging wife" variety. At their core are often legitimate, unresolved issues or concerns that we have discussed before under less stressful circumstances. Sometimes the concerns are about our relationship, but they can as easily be about work, other family members, or something entirely new. No relationship is an island, free from the external pressures and issues of the rest of life. On a two-have-become-one marriage team, what affects one person affects the other. Occasionally, unresolved conflict also contributes to the situation.

I'm lucky. I can predict when Tari is most likely to experience these feelings. Tari's not so lucky. I'm pretty steady, but at times I also get discouraged, sensitive, sad, moody, upset, or argumentative. And I think that's true of most guys, if we're honest. But I can't predict when, and neither can she. It's like the difference between a defense that often blitzes the weak-side linebacker on third-and-long and a defense that can blitz anybody in any situation at any place on the field. One you know *how* to prepare for; the other you always have to *be* prepared for.

If I want to be a good husband, I have to prepare to be one. Part of that preparation involves recognizing situations that can undermine the unity of our team. I have to identify the patterns that hinder my movement toward becoming the kind of husband I want to be. I have to know what the scouting report says about the ways my wife and I express our self-centeredness. First Corinthians 9:24–25, loosely paraphrased and applied specifically to marriage, could read as follows: "Play to win. But in order to play that way, you've got to prepare that way. You've got to faithfully, purposefully, and consistently prepare to play the game. The game we play, the marriage game, is the one that really matters." And if we see our marriages as invaluable tools in our transformation, we can see how much it really does matter.

I now have Tari's period discreetly marked on my calendar to remind me. I am prepared. I know what is likely to happen. I know when it is likely to happen. And I know what I have to do. If she says or does something that hits me in just the wrong way, I know I have to be willing to extend extra grace. Instead of retaliating or escalating the negative tone, I can step back. This doesn't mean I avoid conflict. It means I don't let conflict control my response. I have a responsibility to my teammate.

And by the way, I never, *ever* say, "Oh, come on. It's just because you're having your period." I may know it. And Tari may know it. And we may be able to talk about it reasonably at some other time. But not during. And never with a patronizing or dismissive tone. As I said before, the issues are usually legitimate.

I'm not solely responsible for our harmony. Both of us are responsible for our own actions, or lack of actions, that contribute to a breakdown in our team. Tari has as much responsibility for building our marriage as I do. But I try to play each day in our marriage game as though it starts with me.

"Anticipate and get there"—the two sides of preparation for Mike Singletary.

Anticipation is nothing more than knowing what is likely to happen based on a study of the game. Without knowing what is likely to happen, it doesn't matter how good a player is or what kind of shape he is in; he probably won't be in position to make the play. He'll get there a step late. The game moves too fast in the NFL. That one step could be the difference between making a key third-down tackle that stops a drive or giving up just enough yardage to keep the drive alive.

On the other hand, a linebacker may know his opponent so well you'd think he was in the offense's huddle. But if he doesn't execute, he'll be no more effective than if he hadn't prepared at all. He has to do what he prepared to do, and do it with conviction.

Otherwise, he will be dominated. The athletes are too good. Small disparities in physical abilities or mental preparation can make a huge difference at that level.

One of the principles marital researcher John Gottman discusses in his book *The Seven Principles for Making Marriage Work* is to "enhance your love maps." "Love maps" is Gottman's phrase for knowing what is important to a spouse and what is going on in his or her life. It starts with building a base of background knowledge. But life isn't stagnant. Neither are our wives. We must continually update the information based on the circumstances of their lives that are changing. When we have an accurate, up-to-date picture of our wives and their world, we have the scouting report on their lives. We know what's important to them and why. We're in a better position to serve them.

We have to make it a point to stay connected with our wives. We have to know what's going on in their lives and how they feel. Is there an ongoing issue with a child that they really need our support on? When are they likely to be anxious about a situation at work and need an encouraging hug? Is there something we've done, or not done, that might discourage them? We can reassure them of our commitment by acknowledging it and working to get better. Is there some aspect of their appearance that they are insecure about (and I guarantee you there is), and can we help by telling them that they're attractive? If we're not prepared for those types of circumstances, we're likely to respond by taking the easy way out. Let's face it: our natural inclination is to respond in ways that don't require more emotional energy than we want to give. But if we are prepared, we're likely to respond to the challenges in ways that build our wives up, reinforce their trust in us, and strengthen our marriages.

Of course, our preparation is not just to defend against the threats to our marriages. We've also got to know about the positive things going on. We need to know when our wives are probably going to be excited about some development and will want to talk about it. If they've spent time catching up with a friend, most likely they'll want to share that experience with us. If a child accomplished something we don't know about, they will want to tell us about it. And if we've had an experience without them, they'll feel more connected with us if we discuss it with them.

Tari is a great wife but not a perfect wife. She has shortcomings, and so do I. When she takes steps to grow, I have to affirm her. I have to have my antennae up. If I'm functioning on autopilot, I may miss an opportunity to encourage her.

It's helpful to know that we'll never have home-field advantage in our quest for a Super Bowl marriage. All our games are on the road in our contemporary society. We have to be prepared for the distractions we will face. Much about our world encourages physical pleasure and ego gratification at the expense of true connection. From its obsession with sex to its emphasis on a material lifestyle that requires continual changes and upgrades, our culture can get us off track. The demanding pace of modern life can distract even further. Staying focused on marriage is another challenge we have to prepare for.

The Bears' 46 Defense was an aggressive, attacking defense. They didn't sit back and hope to stop the offense when it showed up. They got after it. They were intelligent and disciplined, but they created chaos for their opponents.

Play fakes, pulling guards, and running backs who were bigger or faster or both—Mike Singletary knew what he was up against. He knew how to prepare. Run the hill, watch the films, make the plays. Prepare the body, prepare the mind, perform the task. Running sprints, watching game film, keeping himself in good mental shape—Singletary understood they were merely investments in success. All the sprints and film study in the world won't prepare him to be a great husband, however.

"If there's one thing that sets me apart, it's attitude," Singletary said, summarizing his football success. "I'm not just talking about desire and dedication. Lots of people have all of that you could ask for. And I'm not just talking about persistence, never-say-die, never give up, though that's a big part of it too. I'm talking about something that includes all that and a lot more. I'm talking about obsession."

Singletary didn't want to run that hill; he had to. Unless we are similarly obsessed with being a great spouse, we won't do the work of preparation. If we don't do the work of preparation, we won't be ready for either the challenges or the opportunities. And if we're not ready for them, even the small daily ones, they're going to blindside us or pass us by before we even know what's going on.

The Extra Point

You're a college linebacker picked in the third round by the Chicago Bears in 1986. Mike Singletary just left a voice mail for you.

"Congratulations! Welcome to the team," he says. "The standard is high around here. If you're serious about this, you'll need to prepare. The team needs you to prepare. Why don't you come by, and I'll show you how I get ready. Workouts, studying film—they'll help you be a better player. If you're serious." You return the call a couple of days later.

"Thanks Mike, but I've been playing the position for four years now. I think I know what I'm doing. Don't worry; we've got time. Minicamps. Training camps. I'll have time to learn."

"Excellence doesn't just happen. If you're not preparing to help the team, you're hurting the team," he responds. "And the sooner you start preparing, the sooner you start helping. If you want to be an All Pro, you have to start preparing to be an All Pro."

—

What can you do to prepare to be the best husband you can possibly be?

What predictable patterns are there in your daily personal and professional life that get in the way of your being a Super Bowl husband?

The Block That Won the Super Bowl

*You can accomplish a lot
if you don't worry about who gets the credit.*

—Bill Arnsparger

The greatest run in the history of the NFL? In 1990, NFL Films decided that honor did not belong to Gale Sayers, the Kansas Comet who tied an NFL record with six touchdowns in one game in his rookie season of 1965. Neither does it belong to Jim Brown, whose career average of 5.22 yards per carry and eight seasons of leading the league in rushing are tops in NFL history.

Eric Dickerson followed his rookie rushing record of 1,808 yards in 1983 with a single-season record of 2,105 in 1984. However, none of the runs in his Hall of Fame career was worthy of the title "greatest." Walter Payton combined speed, strength, durability, and legendary toughness to forge a thirteen-year, 16,726-yard career. But none of his 3,838 rushing attempts was judged to be the greatest.

Sure, it's subjective, but none of those runs captured the hearts of the people at NFL Films in the same way as a broken play in the 1988 season. To be fair, in 1990 Barry Sanders was only a season into a career marked by spectacular runs, and eventual career-rushing leader Emmitt Smith was a rookie. Possibly the greatest run in the history of the NFL was not pulled off by one of the great running backs but by a second-string quarterback who, by the time he retired, had become the league's highest-rated passer, both for a career and a single season. And the final, most devastating block was thrown not by a lineman but by a thin wideout from Mississippi Valley State who had set a single-season record the previous year with an astonishing twenty-two touchdown receptions.

"He's back to throw. He's in trouble. He's about to be sacked," warned the broadcaster. Indeed, the pocket was collapsing so quickly and completely around the quarterback that it would have been difficult to determine who would get credit for the sack. Just over two minutes remained in the game, and the quarterback's team trailed 21–17. Another loss, their fourth in only nine games, might cripple their chances of winning their division or even reaching the playoffs at all.

Football is mostly a workmanlike game of 8-yard receptions and incompletions, 4-yard runs and stops for no gain, ten-play drives and three-and-outs. The Sunday evening sports shows summarize a day's games with highlights. There's a reason they're called highlights. The efforts of two teams for an entire afternoon are reduced to three or four dramatic plays.

However, for every significant completion, there is an offensive line that performs as efficiently, if not as obviously, as the receiver who makes the big catch. Drive-stopping interceptions are often the by-product of a defensive line pressuring the quarterback to throw early. Punts returned for touchdowns are set up by a defense simply holding their opponent to less than 10 yards for three successive plays.

The dramatic is often preceded by the mundane. Players doing nothing more than efficiently performing ordinary tasks will sometimes yield an extraordinary result. Sometimes an extraordinary result will have far-reaching consequences.

Every time the spotlight shines on a single player, his teammates help put him there. Every successful play is a testimony to teammates performing their roles well. A key block can spring a runner for a few more yards. A few more yards might put a runner into a position to break a tackle. A broken tackle might lead to a touchdown. A touchdown might win a game. A single game might be enough to get a team into the playoffs. And the playoffs are the road to the Super Bowl.

The Super Bowl was probably the last thing on the quarterback's mind as the defenders swarmed around him. Suddenly, like a cork in a whirlpool, the quarterback popped free of the churning mass. The tackle, guard, and center had sealed the rush to the inside, allowing the quarterback to duck under and spin out. All that separated him from the go-ahead touchdown were 50 yards and a defense that included five All Pros. Drawing equally on his survival instincts and improvisational skills, he turned upfield.

At the 45, this passer-turned-runner tucked in behind his fullback. Like the sun's rays being focused through a magnifying glass, three defenders converged on the little convoy. The All Pro middle linebacker cut off the quarterback's escape to the outside. The All Pro safety came straight on. Another linebacker closed from the inside. The fullback lunged at the middle linebacker, flew cross-bodied into the safety, and leg whipped the other linebacker. It wasn't a textbook block, and it didn't lay anybody out. But it did slow everybody up, giving the quarterback just enough room to cut back and escape the three-defender pileup.

An All Pro defensive tackle hustled back into the play, too far back into it. He missed the arm tackle, a victim of his own momentum as he slid to the grass. The All Pro cornerback raced up to stop this nonsense before it went any further. He was met with a straight arm. Unable to get his head across his target's body, he bounced harmlessly to the ground as the quarterback continued across the field for a few more yards.

A nifty bit of running, but as the quarterback neared the far sideline at the 30, he saw another defensive back coiled in a perfect tackling stance. The next thing he saw was one of his 270-pound guards veering toward the sideline and the crouching safety. It was more of an obstruction than a block, but effective nonetheless. The defender could only reach toward the quarterback, who once again cut back toward the middle. An 8-yard loss had turned into a 23-yard gain, but he'd probably run a bobbing, weaving, twisting, turning 60 yards. A linebacker was closing on the tiring runner. At the 25, just as the defender started to reach for the quarterback, he was knocked off course by a perfect shoulder-pads-to-chest, downfield block by one of the wideouts.

He turned upfield once again and could see only green grass ahead. What he couldn't see behind him was another linebacker, once again sprinting back into the play. He also couldn't see his other 270-pound guard, also sprinting back into the play, 30 yards from where he had first protected his signal caller. Just like his linemate, he was not in position for a crushing block. He lunged, knocking the linebacker off stride and giving his quarterback a few more yards. And a few yards later, at the 17 to be precise, is where the off-stride linebacker came face to face with the blocker who, the year before, had set the single-season record for touchdown receptions. Wile E. Coyote never came to a more abrupt stop.

At the 15-yard line the quarterback made the mistake of glancing over his shoulder. Spent from the effort, he tripped, then awkwardly stumbled. Alarmingly, he was no longer running but lunging, off balance, head well out in front of his body, hand down in an attempt to steady himself. With a tackler nearly upon him at the 2-yard line, the quarterback dove into the end zone, more a staggering end than a triumphal entry.

The greatest run in the history of the NFL was Steve Young's 1988 scramble against the Vikings. He literally willed himself into the end zone, crossing the goal line for the winning touchdown with 1:58 left in the game. Though Young had the lead role in this twenty-second drama, it was his supporting cast that earned him the Oscar. Without their contributions and willingness to do whatever it took, wherever it had to be done, some other run would have earned that superlative label.

Yes, it was Steve Young's scramble, but it was the selfless blocks of his teammates that made the touchdown possible. The team is what's important. A willingness to do whatever it takes to win the game is what's important. The same is true in marriage.

BLOCKS ON THE MARRIAGE SCRAMBLE

"You're letting a six-pound baby kick your butt," Craig said. As a graduate of the U.S. Naval Academy and a marine jet pilot, he had received similarly candid pep talks himself many times. But these were not the words Donna, his wife, needed to hear. She was struggling in her role as a first-time mom to a newborn.

In three and a half years, she had gone through a rapid succession of changes: from being a single, working professional, living by herself in a beautiful townhouse loft to being a wife, the immediate day-to-day mother for Craig's two children, the proud mother of a baby born five weeks premature, and a woman trying to decide whether to return to work after maternity leave.

Shortly after coming home from the hospital with Erik, Donna found out what really went on in their neighborhood during the day: nothing, nothing at all. Adults went to and from work. Kids went to and from school. It's what Craig did, and it's what the children, Neal and Christy, did. It's not what Donna and Erik did, however. The tornado of change came to an abrupt halt for Donna when it dropped her in her own house to be home alone all day with a crying baby.

All babies cry, but Erik was exceptional. Donna has the personal journal entries to prove it. He cried all day, and Donna felt unqualified, inexperienced, disorganized, and out of control—common feelings among first-time moms. It was the complete opposite of the way she had lived prior to marriage. It was also the loneliest time of her life.

Craig's life continued much the same as before, except he was in a new position at work—a new, demanding position. He was struggling too. He wanted to live out the Galatians 5:13 instruction to "serve one another in love," and he was trying. He'd tried being helpful. He'd asked what he could do. He genuinely wanted to help, but Donna didn't know what to ask for. She was also reluctant to ask. She knew Craig's day was filled with pressure. She felt that she should be able to handle this mom thing. Craig knew she was feeling the stress of the changes in her life. Nothing else had worked, so he took a chance on that more direct approach. It didn't work either.

The stress eventually lessened. Erik began to sleep more and cry less. It had been a difficult four months, but Craig and Donna both acclimated to the changes. The dynamics changed. The pressure abated. The crisis passed. Donna accepted a new position, one every bit as demanding as Craig's new job: she chose to stay home and address the challenges of investing in the development of their children.

Two years later Donna was pregnant again. Shortly after she and Grace, their new daughter, came home from the hospital, Craig had an idea. He had observed how the birth of Erik had affected both of them and the stress it had put on their relationship as they adjusted to the changes. He knew Donna might expect herself to be Supermom again. He knew Donna might experience the very real changes that many women go through following the birth of a child.

Studies estimate that 70 percent to 85 percent of women experience the "baby blues" following the birth of a baby. Hormone levels that dramatically increased during pregnancy suddenly plummet. Changes in hormones produced by a woman's thyroid may lead to her feeling tired, sluggish, and depressed. Additionally, the amount of blood in a woman's body, her blood pressure, immune system, and metabolism all change after pregnancy. Fatigue and mood swings are common results of all the physical changes. Ten percent of women develop some form of postpartum depression.

As a man, Craig knew he wouldn't be able to understand those changes, but he didn't have to in order to prepare for them. He also knew that his "Buck up, marine!" pep talks would be counterproductive.

"What can I do to help? When Grace wakes up in the middle of the night crying, what if I go sit with her?" Craig suggested. He had learned a lot. He knew what to ask. He also knew that Donna, like many spouses, either would be reluctant to ask for his help or wouldn't know what to tell him when he offered. He simply followed his question with a suggestion. He offered a solution to the problem he expected his team would face. He then stated a necessary caveat: "But you're going to have to wake me up, because you know I won't hear her." Apparently, like many other husbands, Craig has a gift for sound sleep. He knew the best thing he could do for his teammate was to offer her sleep. Disrupted sleep is one of the key contributing factors to depression.

Donna had learned a lot too. She knew the wisdom of accepting Craig's offer, even if she still felt a tug of guilt and inadequacy. They were both better prepared for the arrival of Grace. Experience can do that for you, but only if you're willing to learn from it and grow. A deal was struck.

"Serve one another in love." Most weddings refer to that passage. Pastors say it. Husbands and wives commit to it. But how does it play out in the day-to-day life of the marriage? If you're not prepared to see the opportunities, they will pass by you. And if you're not prepared to act on them when you do see them, they will run over you.

"Craig's willingness to get up and do that was *huge*," admitted Donna. "I felt like I didn't have to do it all. I wasn't alone. I had a partner." Donna had a teammate. More important, she had a teammate who understood that preparation was important but that preparation without execution was as bad as no preparation at all.

He also understood that what he was offering wasn't going to make a marriage highlight film. It was a matter of anticipating a need and doing whatever it took to move the team ahead.

"When Steve Young made his incredible 49-yard run" is how Bill Walsh remembered the run. It is an efficient way to describe the play. However, had it not been for the anonymous contributions of his teammates, at best the scramble would have been a resourceful quarterback turning an 8-yard loss into a 3-yard gain. Regardless of his athletic ability and determination, Steve Young would not have scored.

As Young spun free of the collapsing pocket, it was center Randy Cross, guard Guy McIntyre and tackle Harris Barton who sealed the rush to the inside. It was fullback Tom Rathman who slowed the three Vikings just enough at the 45 to allow Young to escape. McIntyre was the first of the guards to rejoin the battle downfield, screening his quarterback from the safety 25 yards from the line of scrimmage. Viking linebacker Chris Martin would have dropped Young at the 25 if a Niner receiver, unidentifiable even in slow motion replays, had not dropped him first. Guard Jesse Sapolu could have stayed near the line of scrimmage as Young headed downfield. Linemen often do, especially late in the game. Instead, it was his lunge at Jesse Solomon, the linebacker closing in on Young from behind at the 20, that set up that final helmet-rattling block. And it was Jerry Rice, the man who would eventually catch more passes for more yards and score more touchdowns than anyone ever had, who braced his feet, lowered his shoulder, and launched into Solomon, bringing a cartoonish stop to the last Minnesota hope of preventing Young from scoring.

Who does the work? Who gets the credit? Who cares? When someone does the work, the team wins. A couple of months later the 49ers won it all but not with Steve Young as quarterback. Though Young had the single most significant play of the 49ers season, he was back on the bench for the Super Bowl. It was Joe Montana who led San Francisco to the win.

Craig and Donna worked out a simple plan in their awake moments, when they could make rational decisions. Instead of playing the "Okay, fine, since you're not going to get up" martyr game when Grace cried at 2:00 a.m., they decided that Craig would answer that call. Ever the marine jet pilot, Craig had his preflight checklist for his time with Grace.

Diaper—check.

Feed her—check.

Burp her—check.

Signs of other discomfort—check.

Swaddle her so she feels secure—check.

Play a Fernando Ortega CD to calm both their spirits—check.

He was usually clear to return to base about 45 minutes later.

Craig knew his early morning sorties wouldn't last forever, but the impact they would have on Donna would. It would also impact him forever as he strengthened a habit of serving both his wife and his daughter. He was prepared to suffer a little sleep deprivation for the sake of his teammate and the good of the team. His preparation was sound, his execution superb.

One block on one play in one game in the middle of the season. Which block was most important? Without *any one* of them, Young doesn't score, the Niners probably lose, and Super Bowl hopes disappear.

There is no end to the "serve one another in love" opportunities in marriage. Though you don't have to look for them—they're all around you—you may have to train yourself to see them. You also may have to train yourself to creatively respond to them. It's a matter of studying your wife, learning about the things that affect her, and staying connected with her life to know how you can serve her.

Steve Young couldn't have known who was doing what on his behalf. The play was developing too rapidly. Only a person willing to study a slow-motion replay of the scramble could identify the players and their contributions. Getting credit was not the point; winning the game was. Life can also develop pretty rapidly. Husbands and wives who don't train themselves to see ways to serve their spouses fail to take advantage of an important tool in their ongoing transformation into more Christlike people.

A husband who is willing to pay the price of preparation and to follow through with executing the solution will win the confidence and trust of his teammate and win the marriage game.

the extra point

The game clock is winding down, and so are your team's chances for victory. The ball is snapped, and you look for the blitzing linebacker. It's your primary responsibility on the play. Here he comes, just as you expected. And you know what's coming. He's going to rush upfield as if he is going to take the outside rush, then suddenly stop, grab your shoulder pads, and get you off balance as he cuts back inside for the sack. It's his favorite move. You've seen it on film, and you're ready.

You stay low and keep your weight back. When he stops, he has to come to you. Your momentum is not his ally as he grabs your pads. You're set. He can't budge you and gets up too high trying. You simply drive into his legs and knock him to the ground. You've won your battle. You've done your job.

But one of your teammates hasn't. Your quarterback is flushed from the pocket and is buying time while scrambling around in the backfield. Do you lie there thinking, *I did my job. Looks like this play is going for a loss. Too bad. This wouldn't be happening if the line had blocked better?*

———

Does your marriage teammate have a need that you can help with, regardless of whose job it is?

If you haven't observed one, ask. She has one or more, whether you realize it or not.

when it mattered most

In the big games, two or three plays
will make the game for you.
—JACK HAM

omewhere between now and the end of the game, somebody's going to make a play and put his team in the Super Bowl," said John Madden as the broadcast of the NFC championship game was resuming after the television time-out.

Improbably, the quarterback and one of his receivers had been standing at their opponents' 30, chatting each other up during the time-out. It was third-and-four with 4:50 left in the game. They had not scored a touchdown all day and trailed 6–5. This drive might be their last chance. A field goal would put them ahead, but a lot can go wrong on a 47-yard field-goal attempt, and they knew it. Besides, a 2-point lead wouldn't exactly be a cushion.

"What if I were to run a hitch?" the receiver had asked during the break. It was a safe suggestion, a high-percentage pattern, certain to get the first down if completed.

"Yeah, or we could go for it all and run a fade," offered the quarterback.

"What do you think?" responded the wideout.

Flex Left Smoke Right 585 H-Choice was the play they would run when the game resumed. It was designed to get the ball to the back coming out of the backfield so he could get the first down. The wide receiver, the second choice on the play, and the quarterback were discussing Plan B. The game was on the line. The season was on the line. If there was ever a time to step up, this was it.

Improbable? After five solid years with the Cardinals, the receiver was with his third team in the last five years. He had been the MVP the year before, *team* MVP on a 4-12 team. With the return to form of an injured veteran and the emergence of younger, faster receivers, his reception total had dropped to thirty-three. For the first time since an injury-hampered 1995 season in which he had caught only five passes, he had failed to score a touchdown.

Improbable? The quarterback was signed as an undrafted free agent by the Green Bay Packers, then cut during training camp in 1994. He'd kicked around the Arena League and NFL Europe, trying to keep his skills sharp for another shot in the NFL. Four years later he finally latched on for an inconsequential season as a backup to the backup. When he finally got his shot, however, he filled the air with footballs. Unfortunately, he had to wait until the last 3:38 of the last game of the season to get that shot. He completed only four of the eleven passes he threw, none for touchdowns. Prior to the start of the current season, his résumé was a little thin.

Improbable? Two years before, the head coach had been hired to lead the team to the promised land of the Super Bowl. He'd done it once, but only once, nineteen years before. First, he had to lead the 6-10 team to respectability. Like a lot of turnaround projects, things went from bad to worse, however. They corkscrewed right into the NFL cellar with 5-11 and 4-12 seasons. The trend was not encouraging.

Improbable? The former backup to the backup put together one of the finest seasons in NFL history and earned league MVP honors. His total of forty-one touchdown passes was the third highest in NFL history, and his quarterback rating of 109.2 was fifth best.

"The greatest single-season sports story in history" is how ESPN's Chris Berman described the quarterback's season.

Improbable? The team finished the season with an NFC-best 13-3 record. They were fast, balanced, deep, aggressive, and, most important, productive. Their total of 526 points, an average of 33 a game, was the third highest in NFL history. They had maintained form in the divisional playoffs the week before by hanging 49 points on their opponents.

Improbable? This irresistible-force offense had managed but one field goal in this game for the conference championship. They had met their match in the immovable-object defense of their opponents. Three points in fifty-five minutes of football. The high-octane offense appeared out of gas, their MVP sputtering.

His first pass of the game was intercepted. On his team's second possession, he drove them to a first-and-goal from the 6-yard line.

But he misfired on two passes before a fumbled hand-off forced them to kick a field goal. He drove the team to the 9 in the third quarter. After a 15-yard penalty moved them back to the 24, his next pass was intercepted at the 4, killing the drive. He had thrown only thirteen interceptions in the entire regular season, but he threw his third of the game later in the quarter. It looked as if he might be choking in the biggest game of his life, but nearly five minutes were still left.

"Let's go for it," said the quarterback to his receiver. "We need a big play, so what the heck? If they blitz, go deep, and I'm coming to you."

The scouting report had prepared the quarterback for the possibility that the defense might blitz in situations like this. And as the ball was snapped, they did. The receiver saw the blitz and did as he had been told. He knew he'd have single coverage. The cornerback went with him, stride for stride down the left sideline. The offensive tackle picked up the blitzing defender. But the defensive end looped around and found himself with an unobstructed path to the quarterback. He was closing fast. The quarterback hung in the pocket as long as he could, then stepped just as the defensive end launched toward him, and arced a high toss about 40 yards downfield where he hoped the receiver could catch it. Courtesy of the defensive end, he then took a seat at the 40 in an obstructed-view section—behind more than a ton of thrashing linemen.

Down the sideline went the receiver and the defensive back, step for step, eyes locked on the ball spiraling toward them. The back reached out his left hand to feel the wideout as he continued to sprint while looking back over his right shoulder. The receiver reached as well, parrying the defender with his right hand, as they both raced toward the end zone.

The receiver leaned back into the defender as both went up for the ball at the 2-yard line. For a fraction of a second, it looked as though the receiver had made the catch. Then, with the sideline only a foot away, the ball started to pop loose. Desperately, the wideout curled his left arm around the ball while still elbowing the defender with his right. He hugged the ball to his chest, a snow cone of brown leather, then secured it with his right hand as he tumbled to the ground.

Picturesque? No.

Improbable? Yes.

Touchdown? Yes!

"That's *a* play," Madden deadpanned.

When it mattered most, with time winding down in what could have been the last game of a dream season, St. Louis Rams quarterback Kurt Warner, the former backup to the backup, stepped into the teeth of the rush and threw a perfect pass.

When it mattered most, Ricky Proehl, the ten-year veteran, the former team MVP who had been "reduced" to the team's fifth leading receiver, the perfectly covered second choice on the play, made the catch of his life.

When it mattered most, the upstart St. Louis Rams, a 4-12 cellar dweller the year before, did what they had to do and pulled out an 11–6 victory over the Tampa Bay Buccaneers in the NFC championship game.

WHEN IT MATTERS MOST IN MARRIAGE

And when does it matter most in marriage? When is it especially important for the husband and wife, teammates on this marriage team, to rise to the challenge and do what's necessary to win the game?

"Contrary to popular belief, it's not how much you love each other that can best predict the future of your relationship, but how conflicts and disagreements are handled," say marital researchers and therapists Howard Markman, Scott Stanley, and Susan Blumberg. Conflict situations are when it matters most in marriage.

Note that they do not say "how conflicts and disagreements are resolved." Very often the differences that cause conflict may be unresolvable. Research done by John Gottman indicates that 69 percent of a couple's conflicts fall into a category he calls "perpetual." Perpetual problems don't get resolved. A couple can learn to identify areas of conflict and engage in respectful discussions about them. That's great. That's necessary for a marriage to grow. But Gottman's data indicates that almost seven out of ten issues a couple faces this year will be faced again next year and the next and the next.

It's a challenge to resolve conflict in marriage. But it can be even more challenging to protect the harmony of your relationship from the effects of conflicts that don't get resolved. Harmony is not the false peace that results when a husband or wife looks the other way and pretends not to notice or be bothered by a partner's behavior. It's not the "everything's okay" illusion that many people strive for.

The harmony we're striving for is much harder to achieve. It's also much more nourishing and rewarding. It is our respect for each other. It's our loving acceptance of each other, in spite of our flaws. It's agreeing on the direction and purpose of the marriage. And it's unity in pursuit of that purpose. That's what we're talking about.

Conflict is the natural and inevitable result of any two people working together. And often the closer we work with someone and the harder we work on something together, the more opportunity there is for conflict. When two people come together and form a marriage team, they bring with them personality differences. Gender differences. Differences in families of origin. Life-experience differences. Differences in needs and expectations. Differences in the way they communicate. Differences in parenting approaches, if they have children. And other differences too numerous to mention. Those differences will generate a certain amount of conflict. That is one thing in marriage you can count on with absolute certainty.

Conflict often feels like a blitz to me. A lot is happening emotionally, and it's happening quickly. Much like a quarterback, I often feel exposed, vulnerable to the pain or embarrassment that can happen. My natural instinct is to protect myself. Forget the play; it's a matter of survival. At least that's what it often feels like.

Kurt Warner wasn't rattled by Tampa Bay's blitz. He knew he was at risk. And he knew he had to get rid of the ball before he got drilled. But he expected a blitz and knew it was intended to hurry him into doing something stupid or careless. He also knew that when the game was most chaotic and he was most in danger, he had to perform at his best. Conflict creates those times in marriage. You either rise to the challenge or yield to your instinct to protect yourself.

Conflict doesn't necessarily mean that something bad is happening. When conflict arises, someone may not be right and someone may not be wrong. It's very possible you will find two people who are just different. And different may mean you both have to grow. If handled well, it could be a catalyst for individual growth and for strengthening the relationship. It has become a catalyst in my marriage to Tari.

In the spirit of "the *I* in team," I had to look at how I was handling conflict in my marriage compared to what I was learning in books like *Fighting for Your Marriage, The Seven Principles for Making Marriage Work, Love and Respect,* and others.

Was I insightful enough to identify the sources and circumstances of the conflict I felt?

Was I honest enough to accept responsibility for the contribution I was making to conflict situations?

Was I wise enough to see that the catalyst for a specific conflict might be only an indication of a deeper, unmet need for love, respect, or acceptance?

Was I persistent enough to look for that true catalyst, especially if the search turned up at my door?

Was I trusting enough that I could initiate a respectful discussion in which I honestly discussed, without judging or accusing, how I felt as a result of some conflict we were experiencing?

Did I have the courage to listen without interrupting in order to understand Tari and how the situation affected her rather than to listen in order to prepare a defense and win a point?

Did I have the confidence and poise necessary to speak in ways that communicated love, respect, and an unshaken commitment to the marriage in spite of how I felt at the time?

Regardless of how chronic and frustrating the conflict might be, was I so focused and purposeful that I refused to let it undermine my own pursuit of Christlikeness?

It's unlikely that any one conflict will destroy your marriage. But how you approach the process of managing it is a good indicator of which needs you are putting first, yours or those of your team. Effectively handling conflict is critical because conflict is one place where a sense of entitlement can be especially aroused.

I know how important it is to handle conflict constructively. I didn't in my first marriage. We didn't outright fight, but each of us had disappointments and unmet needs and expectations. And our differentness resulted in predictable conflict. I often failed even to acknowledge it. I thought I was doing the right thing by stuffing my disappointment, frustration, or anger. I didn't want to be thought of as needy or complaining. I thought I was being a hero by not bringing things up. I realize now I was just avoiding it, taking the easy way out, and serving myself. I also realize how destructive it was to my relationship. And I certainly didn't have the skills needed to deal with conflict.

In their book *Fighting for Your Marriage,* Markman, Stanley, and Blumberg identify four negative patterns of handling conflict: escalation, invalidation, withdrawal and avoidance, and negative interpretation. Before we learned how to constructively deal with the conflict that naturally occurred in our relationship, Tari and I had all four covered.

I placed a high value on peace. It's consistent with my temperament. Unfortunately, it wasn't true, healthy peace. It wasn't the peace that results from two people talking about, understanding, and respecting each other's differences. It wasn't the harmony that results when two people commit to improving the relationship. It was more of an absence of verbalized feelings, a false, short-term peace. Classic avoidance.

It's also the "training" I had received in my family as I grew up. Conflict was rarely discussed or constructively handled. My mom and dad hadn't known how to handle their differences other than to suppress them quickly. Nobody taught them to do otherwise. And let's face it, handling conflict productively is almost impossible to learn on your own. So I learned to avoid conflict. It was easy. The training I received fit naturally with how I was wired. I grew up believing that conflict meant the relationship was in trouble.

Tari's family had no such problems, however. She came from a family in which disappointment and conflict were openly, if not constructively, acknowledged. If one family member had a problem with another family member, it was shared, often in sharp, accusing tones. Far from being suppressed, the conflict usually escalated as the other family member responded in kind. Avoiding conflict or aggressively engaging in it were not isolated situations. They were entrenched relationship patterns in our families. It's the way our parents related to each other. Not surprisingly, it's the way Tari and I learned to deal with conflict.

Terry, the conflict avoider who often "heard" things that weren't being said, married Tari, the experienced infighter who knew not only how to survive conflict but how to "win" with verbal barbs. It was a perfect match of equally destructive approaches, and our relationship suffered for a long time.

Tari would say or do something that I perceived as a put-down. Sometimes it truly was a put-down, but much more often it was a matter of my negative interpretation. Rather than make the effort to clarify what she meant, I would withdraw. Sometimes I would physically withdraw and leave the house. More often than not, my withdrawal was emotional as I would simply disengage with a comment like "Fine" and turn cold. Tari would pursue. Eventually, if she cornered me, I would feel provoked and respond angrily.

"Don't make a big deal out of this," she'd chide. Invalidation.

"Okay, fine," I'd say, nodding as I put up an emotional wall. It was my dad's response. In my case, it represented an unwillingness to deal with conflict in healthy ways. I was withdrawing from the conflict. I was also withdrawing from the relationship. And as I did, I took with me any positive feelings, the feelings necessary for the relationship to grow, the feelings Tari needed. Our conflict-management skills were not well developed. In fact, they stunk.

There was also a time when Kurt Warner's pocket discipline stunk. "Whenever there was any pressure at all I'd bail out of the pocket and start running all over the place," he recalls of his freshman year in high school, his first as a quarterback. So his coach came up with a fun little drill called "Kill Kurt." At the snap of the ball, the defensive linemen would crash into the offensive linemen as they rushed Warner. But he wasn't allowed to throw the ball. All he could do was move around *in the pocket* until a defender beat his man and nailed him. Stay in the pocket and take the hits. What a great way to spend your freshman year.

"I can't overstate how much I hated this," Warner says. "But here's the thing: it made me a better player, and it formed good habits that are still with me today. Now one of my strong suits is that I stand there under pressure and deliver the ball accurately, even if someone's in my face and I'm about to take a shot." Warner learned early how to overcome his fears. He could then focus on becoming a more effective quarterback.

Any husband and wife who want to become a more effective marriage team will have to learn conflict management skills. Most of the time, Tari's and my marriage went along very smoothly. It would have looked like a flourishing relationship to an outsider. In many ways it was, but our marriage could advance no further and in fact would probably have begun to erode had we both not learned to deal constructively with conflict.

We started to put our marriage ahead of our individual discomfort, and we knew we had to do this differently—different from the marriages we grew up seeing, different from the way we'd been doing it. It started with each of us honestly assessing our own negative patterns. Tari admitted that she had learned escalation in her family and that she brought it into our marriage. The survival skills of invalidation she had developed as a child would always stand in the way of having the marriage she wanted.

I recognized how reluctant I was to bring up conflict. I also knew that the short-term peace I was settling for hurt my long-term relationship. It had happened in my first marriage, and now it was affecting my second. I could see that my habit of negative interpretation wasn't fair to Tari and would always hold me back in developing as a husband.

Many of our initial attempts at conflict resolution were awkward. But we both drew encouragement from each other's willingness to try something difficult. We got caught in an upward spiral. We were encouraged by each other's commitment to the team and willingness to grow. We gave each other the benefit of the doubt instead of assuming the worst. That led to increased trust and an even stronger commitment to the team and growth. Our skills improved. Our confidence in ourselves and each other grew. It was classic team building, and it took time, but we had momentum on our side.

One day I discovered an unexpected residue of conflict. An issue came up in which Tari disappointed me. She had dropped the ball. We had a productive, respectful discussion about it, and then I left to run some errands. Happy ending, right? Maybe not.

As I was out, I noticed how I was looking at women. I'd see an attractive woman and think, *I bet she wouldn't treat me like that. I deserve better than this.* It pretty quickly got to, *I wonder what it would be like to be with her?* I normally don't let myself think like that. Clearly I was choosing to ignore the "is not self-seeking," "does not delight in evil," "always protects," "always perseveres," and "never fails" parts of 1 Corinthians 13.

I was planting the seeds of resentment and lustful thinking. I was abandoning a critical marriage principle because I felt entitled. In the process I was undermining the foundation of trust necessary for our team to move ahead. It would have hurt Tari if she had known the way I was looking at and thinking about other women. It certainly would have hurt me if I had discovered she was looking at other men that way. But the conflict had been "her fault," and I felt justified in my entitlement. We always do.

Research done by Robert Levenson and Loren Carter at the University of California indicates that men and women physically respond differently to stress. When a man and a woman are exposed to the same kind of stress, the man's heart rate and blood pressure become more elevated, and they remain so for a longer time. Regardless of appearances to the contrary, many men feel stress more acutely.

In *The Seven Principles for Making Marriage Work,* John Gottman and Nan Silver say these physical differences are exacerbated by the tendency of many men to relive the conflict and hold on to negative thoughts. Women are more likely to have "soothing thoughts" that help them recover from the situation and attempt to restore harmony.

After admitting there was conflict and taking productive steps to work through it, I found I had to choose to forgive Tari. If I didn't forgive her, I couldn't move on, and I certainly couldn't expect her to forgive me when I made mistakes. Without forgiveness, how could I possibly tell myself I was developing a more Christlike character? Without forgiveness, we couldn't build the trust and confidence in each other necessary to win the marriage game. At best, our marriage would remain exactly where it was. More likely though, it would begin to erode as trust disappeared.

The Extra Point

Kurt Warner comes over to you during the time-out. "Marshall (Faulk) is the first choice on this play, but they might be coming. If they do, take off. Expect the ball. We need this. This is what it's all about." He smiles.

"You haven't thrown to me much all year. You already overthrew me once in this game and underthrew me another time. You've thrown three interceptions. It's your fault we're behind. Now you want me to come through for you. I'm going to have to think about it," you respond.

"Think about it? C'mon, I know I'm not having a good game.

That's why I need you to come through. Be there if I need you. You always have been. Our team needs you now. I need you now. Winning the game, getting to the Super Bowl—that's what's important, not who's having a good game and who's having a bad game. Whatever it takes to get this thing done! Right?"

———

Do you engage in any of the negative patterns of escalation, invalidation, withdrawal and avoidance, or negative interpretation when conflict occurs in your marriage?

Do your attitude and behavior build team trust and move you toward the goal or undermine trust and keep you from moving ahead?

the only thing that's constant

The question becomes "What do we need to do differently to keep pace?" Change too little and you get left behind. Change too much and you veer off course.

—Marty Schottenheimer

I say Chuck Noll. You say…Terry Bradshaw.

I say Bill Walsh. You say…Joe Montana.

I say Bill Belichick. You say…Tom Brady.

Those are three of the four head coaches, and their starting quarterbacks, who have won at least three Super Bowls.

The fourth coach? Hmmm. How about a clue? Three Super Bowl championships in ten years with three different starting quarterbacks. Only one coach has done it. And it all had a rather strange beginning.

"You need to get me back there," said the running back to the coach who had come to visit him at his Kansas farm. "I'll make you famous."

I'll get him back and I'll trade him, thought the coach. *I'm not putting up with a fruitcake.*

The coach had recently been named head coach, the first time he had held that position at any level. One of the first changes he sought to make was to persuade the iconoclastic running back to rejoin the team. The back chose to sit out the entire 1980 season in a contract dispute. He wanted to play again but would only do so with a no-trade clause in his contract. The team blinked in this game of contract chicken, agreed to his request, and the first-year coach had an important part of the offense he envisioned.

"I'm bored. I'm broke. I'm back," announced the running back to reporters at the start of training camp.

It wasn't exactly Douglas MacArthur's triumphant return to the Philippines, but neither was the start of the '81 season. The team lost its first five games, and six of their first seven. They were stronger on the back nine, winning seven of those games but still not making the playoffs.

They finished the strike-shortened 1982 season with an 8-1 record, the NFL's best, but they weren't a dominating team. Four of their eight victories were decided by less than a touchdown. Their victories were so fragile that the place-kicker—the *place-kicker*—was named MVP! Not team MVP—league MVP. Of all the men who passed and ran and blocked and tackled, men who risked the end of their professional lives on every play, this contact-avoiding, ten-play-a-game microspecialist was deemed most valuable.

"Load up the wagon. I'm going to carry it," said the running back to the coach prior to first playoff game. He carried the ball twenty-five times for 119 yards in their first-round win, thirty-seven times for 185 yards in their second, and thirty-six times for 140 yards in the game that sent them to the Super Bowl for the second rematch in the game's history.

He carried the ball thirty-eight times for 166 yards and earned the Super Bowl MVP award. His 43-yard touchdown run on fourth-and-one put his team ahead for good. He had delivered on his promises to carry the wagon and make the second-year coach famous.

"The truly great people in this profession are great for years and years," said the coach in the afterglow of the Super Bowl win. "Let's see how I am in ten years."

It's one thing to reach the NFL's mountaintop. It's another to stay there. The coach's team returned to the Super Bowl the following year but lost 38–7. They went from Super Bowl winners in '82 to Super Bowl losers in '83 to divisional playoff losers in '84 to missing the playoffs altogether in '85.

The team that took the field for the beginning of the '86 season was on the rise again. They had absorbed the changes of retirement, injuries, and trades. The quarterback had been thrust into the spotlight after a gruesome injury on *Monday Night Football* ended the starter's career in 1985. He was growing into the role of offensive leader. He guided his team to a 12-4 record and two playoff victories before losing in the conference championship.

The 1987 season was one of chaos. Due to injuries, ineffectiveness, and a players' strike, three different quarterbacks started games. The team finished 11-4, but the inconsistency at quarterback showed. They won both playoff games, although they dominated neither. They spotted the Bears two touchdowns but came back to win 21–17. The winning score came on a 52-yard, third-quarter punt return. They escaped with a 17–10 victory the following week when the punt-return hero once again rose to the occasion by batting away a fourth-down pass at their goal line with less than a minute to play.

They had earned a return to the Super Bowl. Barely.

"I don't have to play well for us to win," said the quarterback prior to the game. "What I have to do is not beat [us] by throwing interceptions or turning the ball over."

They entered the game as underdogs and quickly fell behind 10–0. Near the end of the first quarter, the quarterback dropped back to pass and slipped as he set to throw, straining his knee. He tried to return to the huddle but collapsed. The man who had begun the season as the starter came in and immediately took a sack and threw an incompletion. The stage was set for a long afternoon.

And by the end of the second quarter, the game was over. It was one of the most devastating blowouts in Super Bowl history. The quarterback had returned. He hadn't come this far to sit on the bench in the biggest game of his life. He had to give it another shot. By the time the smoke cleared and he took a knee to close the half, his opponents were in shock. In nineteen plays and only 5:54 of actual time of possession, the NFC team had put up 35 unanswered points and had 356 yards of total offense. The quarterback had completed nine of eleven passes for 228 yards and four touchdowns. He had led his team to a 42–10 victory and was named MVP.

Another season. Another quarterback. Another Super Bowl win.

They slipped off the mountaintop again the next year, dropping to 7-9. Some transitions you can plan for; others are dumped on you. By virtue of injuries and inconsistency, yet another quarterback was given a shot as the starter. The team returned to form with a 10-6 record in '89 but didn't make the playoffs. They returned to the playoffs in 1990 with another 10-6 season. Though they lost 28–10 to San Francisco, the quarterback was developing and the team was jelling.

They came up big in 1991. They reeled off eleven straight victories before losing by a field goal. They finished the season 14-2 and led the league in scoring. Unlike the Super Bowl years of '82 and '87, they did not eke out victories. They won seven games by three touchdowns or more. Their average margin of victory was 19 points in the regular season. They dispatched their playoff opponents with ease, 24–7 and 41–10, to earn yet another trip to the Super Bowl.

After trading turnovers and miscues in a scoreless first quarter, they scored 17 points in the second to take a 17–0 lead at the half. They put the game away with another touchdown only sixteen seconds into the third quarter. The final score of 37–24 does not reflect their dominance.

Another quarterback. Another Super Bowl win.

"Let's see how I am in ten years," the coach had said after the victory in 1983. In 1992, a year ahead of his prescient standard, the Redskins' Joe Gibbs joined Bill Walsh and Chuck Noll as a three-time Super Bowl winner. Bill Belichick would join the group with a victory in Super Bowl XXXIX. But Gibbs is still the only head coach to have done it with three different starting quarterbacks.

In 1983 it was Joe Theismann who handed off the ball to Super Bowl MVP John Riggins thirty-eight times in their victory over Miami. In 1988 it was Doug Williams who lit up the Denver Broncos for those 35 second-quarter points en route to earning his MVP award. By 1992, the reins of the Redskins were in the capable hands of Mark Rypien, who also responded with an MVP performance. Three Super Bowl championships, three different starting quarterbacks. Joe Gibbs adapted to the changes.

CHANGES IN THE MARRIAGE GAME

Brad and Laura handled the first change with ease, though many teams don't. They had been building a relationship for years and developing their skills, so the ease of their transition shouldn't have come as a surprise. One stage had ended, and another had begun.

In his book *Managing Transitions: Making Sense of Life's Changes,* William Bridges identifies three stages of transition: (1) an ending, followed by (2) a period of confusion and stress that he calls "the neutral zone," which is followed by (3) a new beginning. Bridges also distinguishes between change, a situational shift, an alteration in the external circumstances, and transition—the process of letting go of the way things used to be and taking hold of the new. It's an internal adjustment. "Transition is the way we all come to terms with change," says Bridges.

"We were like two teenagers playing house" is how Brad recalls his first year of marriage to Laura. "So grown up, yet so irresponsible." Of course, they weren't much beyond teenagers. Laura was only twenty when they married, Brad a worldly twenty-two.

Marriage is a change, an alteration in the external circumstances. Many couples struggle in that first year when they begin to share not only their lives and living space with someone else but also, and perhaps more important, their expectations of their spouse. They experience a change and often haven't made the transition to the new realities of the day-to-day life of marriage.

Because of the genuine friendship that had always characterized their relationship, Brad and Laura made the transition to husband and wife with only a few minor adjustments. Shortly after Laura graduated from college, they made another change in their circumstances. They left Kansas and moved to Chicago. It was another transition made without great difficulty. Though they didn't know it at the time, it would be their last easy one.

They made career choices. They made sacrifices for the sake of their marriage team. They served together at their church and participated in a small group. They went through a miscarriage. They did life together and learned a lot about each other. They invested themselves in building a great marriage relationship, and they succeeded.

"Our life was so nice, and all of a sudden it was ripped…" Laura paused to consider her word choice.

"It was over," Brad filled in, smiling at the memory.

"It *was* over," Laura continued. "Life as we knew it was over."

Brad and Laura were reflecting on the impact of Katy, one of the sweetest six-year-olds you could ever meet. However, until the six-month mark, she was the personification of Bridges' second stage of transition: a period of confusion and stress. It's funny how the stable, orderly, predictable world of two adults can be turned upside down by a seven-pound baby. But it wasn't funny then as both Laura and Brad struggled to adapt to their new roles.

Brad and Laura married early, had children late, and built an enviable marriage in between. For them, this new season of life wasn't just an ending; it was a loss. The twelve-year relationship they describe as "awesome" and "totally a blast" was as gone as sleeping in on Saturday mornings. You can anticipate how change will affect you, but until the change has actually occurred, you simply don't know.

They faced transitions as individuals and as a couple. Katy was the first domino to fall, an agent of change that set many others in motion. Brad, the more introverted of the two, experienced the loss of Laura as his best friend. Though she was still physically present, she was now consumed by her new role as mother. She wasn't as available for him. The freedom to devote themselves to each other was gone.

They had decided that Laura would stay home with the baby rather than return to her job as a legal assistant. Laura, the extrovert, faced the loss of adult interaction at work and the freedom to connect with Brad and her network of friends. Their expenses increased because of Katy, and at the same time their income decreased.

Brad and Laura were reeling with the suddenness and significance of the changes. Like many first-time parents who have spent nine months getting comfortable with the idea of having a child, they were surprised by how consuming a newborn can be. Transition begins with an ending. Brad and Laura experienced the end of the relationship they had known. They had chosen to have a child. And now? Well, welcome to parenthood. They had to let go of the idea that life would ever be the same.

Life as they knew it *was* over. But life as it could be? Maybe better. Maybe worse. They'd have to decide which. When change happens, we have to take intentionality to a new level. We should anticipate that we'll feel our needs more acutely than before, and so will our wives. During change it's easy to lose sight of serving one another in love. Brad and Laura entered Bridges' second stage of transition: the neutral zone. This is a period of confusion and stress as the impact of the change becomes apparent. Old patterns are disrupted, and a person's way of looking at the world, including himself, is challenged.

Change. Ah, what a great opportunity to learn. Of course, you have to have the patience to look around. Discernment is also helpful, to recognize the impact the changes are having. Courage is a must. You'll need it to honestly face some things about yourself and your wife that you'd rather not know, things that might make your life and marriage more challenging.

One of the things you're bound to learn in a time of change is how strong your self-centeredness really is. There is nothing like a time of change and the stress that often accompanies it to tempt us to focus on ourselves. How we long for that path of least resistance.

But if we have patience, discernment, courage, and a work ethic, we can reap the rewards of discovery. As we discover, we can adapt to the changes. And as we adapt, we can move on to a new beginning. Unfortunately, life does not wait for us to adapt, to completely figure out the new realities. Those experiencing the change have to be intentional about doing the work of transition. If they don't, they are in for a lifetime of confusion or dissatisfaction as the pace of change accelerates.

That's how an individual experiences change and then transitions to what is new. But a marriage is two individuals. Spouses have to adapt to the change themselves. They also have to adapt to how the change affects their partner and their relationship. To transition as individuals is one thing; to transition as a couple is another.

How we respond to change either builds our confidence in each other or erodes it. It might be a little or it might be a lot, but it will be either-or. Only if spouses have developed the habit of seeking to understand their partners will they be able to make a successful transition as a couple. What has enabled Brad and Laura's relationship to experience the change and make the transition? It's their determination to not only know what is going on in the other's life but to understand the impact.

"We were in it together, and it was bad for both of us" is how Laura remembers that time. She wasn't feeling sorry for herself or fixing blame. Brad and Laura allowed Katy to consume them. They were parenting novices, and it showed. The change happened quickly. The transition took time, but they made it.

Joe Gibbs saw a bigger picture than a single Super Bowl win. A win was great. And a single season is a consuming focus. It has to be. But he wanted to put his team in a position to win the Super Bowl every season. Whether his quarterback was Theismann, Williams, or Rypien, he had to figure out ways to win with who he had.

You will have seasons of your married life, though they won't be as clearly defined as an NFL season. Newlyweds, first-time parents, parents of multiple children, parents of school-aged children, empty nesters—regardless of the season, you'll have to figure out ways to win the marriage game.

Though children will have the most profound effect on our marriages, there are other changes. Changes in our careers, our family of origin, where we live, our health, our relationships, and our churches can all have significant impact on our lives and marriages.

Brad and Laura didn't want Katy to be an only child. But, oh what a surprise when child number two became numbers two *and* three. The house they had moved into for their family of four, the car they had purchased for their family of four, the life they envisioned for their family of four... Well, some changes are planned, and others are thrust upon you.

Brad and Laura's former relationship was a memory by the time the twins arrived. But it also provided the foundation for the marriage they continued to build. Jack and Luke brought their own set of challenges, but the hard work of transition had been with Katy. Brad and Laura were more experienced parents and more experienced marriage partners. There's a confidence that comes with making it through challenges together. They knew they could make the necessary transition so their marriage would continue to grow.

A solid marriage was more important than ever before. They understood that their relationship was the emotional environment they provided for their children. It is no less important than the physical environment. Children learn so much about themselves, their world, and relationships from their parents. An important part of being a good parent is being a good spouse.

Brad and Laura are intentional about understanding each other's world. He calls her from work about 7:30 every morning to find out how her day is going. He calls on the way home at night to find out how the day has gone. It is his scouting report on what he might face when he gets home. It helps him prepare himself emotionally. He knows that though his professional day is behind him, he will not head home and relax. They have developed a strong relationship work ethic.

"Date night? C'mon, we lived date night," Brad jokes. Now they live *for* date night. It is the highlight of their week, a chance for them to connect when they still have energy for each other. They are very purposeful about it. They adore their children, but they also cherish their time together. They understand they are in a season of life when their children's needs dominate. That's parenthood. But they also know how important it is to continue to build their marriage. "We work really, really, really hard at trying to look at the other person, what's going on in his day and life and trying to encourage each other," says Laura.

"It's not so much an event. It's an ongoing behavior," adds Brad.

"It's a state of mind, to look at the other person," continues Laura. The habit is so well formed that she admits, "We're to the place now where it doesn't even feel like work."

That's important. Change does happen. External circumstances do change. And it can start to feel chaotic. Marriage teammates can begin to feel like their connection is weakening. Not necessarily divided but not necessarily connected, either. A husband or wife can feel left behind. And that's when our self-centeredness will start chipping away at us.

That's why it's crucial for both of you to develop the skills of transition before you face the big changes.

A football team can win the league championship one season and be a Super Bowl team. Not so with a Super Bowl marriage. A Super Bowl marriage adapts to the changing circumstances over a lifetime. A critical component of a Super Bowl marriage is its ability to transition, to experience the changes that are thrust upon it, and to continue to strive for and reach the goal.

In 2004, after an eleven-year absence from the NFL, Joe Gibbs returned to coaching. Four Super Bowl wins with four different quarterbacks? It's certainly a possibility. But the game has changed. Salary caps. Free agency. Rule changes. A new generation of players. And other changes too numerous to mention. Everyone's watching to see how Gibbs transitions.

Brad is forty; Laura's thirty-eight. Both sets of parents are still alive. Katy is six, Jack and Luke are two. A staggering number of variables await them, changes and transitions that will never end. The only thing they can be certain about is that their lives will change. But they are no longer rookies. They've experienced change. And they've chosen to make the necessary transition so their marriage will continue to thrive, even if it is different than it used to be.

Life is change. Marriage is change. Change happens. Transitions, however, are made. They are an ongoing series of choices made to meet the challenge of change. When two individuals commit their lives to their team and teammate, seek to understand what their teammate is experiencing, and choose to live out that understanding with a 1 Corinthians 13 approach, they can survive change. Not only can they survive, they can thrive. And if they do, they can become more like Jesus in the process. They can win the marriage game.

the extra point

Coach Gibbs is kicking off training camp. You're the defending champions, but there have been a lot of changes: trades, retirement, veteran players trying to come back after injuries, and newly drafted players trying to make an impact. A new team. A new season.

"Everybody's after us," says Gibbs. "Everyone's going to play their best against us. Riggins is back in Kansas, this time for good." He smiles at the memories of the "fruitcake" MVP carrying his team to a Super Bowl win.

"You guys are going to have to step up. We're not the same team we were, but we're still the champions, and we can still win it. You guys know how, but it's up to you. This year is not last year. If you choose to adapt, you'll give us a shot. If you play it the same, we'll be sitting at home watching the playoffs."

—

Careers. Kids. Health. What changes has your relationship experienced, or what changes are you experiencing now?

In terms of your effectiveness as a husband, are you adapting to changes or getting left behind?

The Drive

When we struggle it is more a lack of concentration
than anything else.
—Troy Aikman

e never stop working on the fundamentals—drops, protection pockets, where to go when the pocket breaks. We don't leave all that stuff in training camp," the quarterback had said at the beginning of his third NFL season, the first as a full-time starter.

Eight years and two Super Bowl victories later, nothing had changed.

First-and-ten, ball on their own 8-yard line, trailing 16–13. Behind them were the typical rigors of a preseason, a demanding sixteen-game regular season, two win-or-go-home playoff victories and now the first fifty-seven minutes of the Super Bowl. The success of their entire season would be measured by their performance in the next three minutes and ten seconds. The offense trotted onto the field, knowing they needed to move the ball about 65 yards, to their opponent's 25, for a good shot at a game-tying field goal.

Of course, a field goal was no sure thing. Earlier in the game they had set a Super Bowl record for the shortest missed field goal—after a first-half drive stalled at the 2-yard line. In the fourth quarter the kicker had missed another as his 49-yard attempt sailed wide right.

Veteran teams who have built their poise, confidence, and trust in each other one series at a time over the years understand that three minutes and ten seconds is more than enough time. Even with so little time left in the season, the game is still played one play at a time, one block at a time. Each teammate concentrates on what he has to do, in spite of the pressure, the distractions, and the obstacles. And he trusts his teammates to do the same.

"Get the ball to somebody who can keep it moving forward," is how the quarterback described the team's two-minute offense. It was not based on Hail Mary passes or trick plays but on plays the players knew and constantly practiced.

As the quarterback dropped back on the first play, he saw the linebacker pick up the tight end. He knew the back circling out of the backfield would be open underneath. He threw. The completed pass gained 8 yards. Nothing unusual. The back was the team's leading receiver, number seven in the league.

The tight end was covered on the second play, but the quarterback put it where only his man could make the catch. With a linebacker climbing over his back, the tight end caught it at his shoe tops for a first down. The third play of the drive was another pass that gained 8 yards before the wide receiver, the eventual Super Bowl MVP, scooted out of bounds to stop the clock.

Second-and-two at their own 30 with 2:38 remaining. The back took the hand-off but was only able to get back to the line of scrimmage. The clock ticked down—2:04, 2:03, 2:02, 2:01—to the 2:00 warning. They had picked up only 22 yards in 1:10.

The quarterback went to the sideline to confer with the head coach. There were two minutes left in the game—their third Super Bowl together—and two minutes left in their season. Though the quarterback didn't know it, there were two minutes left in their player-coach relationship. The coach had already decided to retire after the game but had decided to wait until the season ended to announce his plans. The team needed to focus on the game, not the end of an era.

Two minutes. Time to start putting up the long ball? Not with three time-outs and a team full of veterans. They calmly stuck to their usual approach and kept looking for opportunities to keep the ball moving. The running back had fumbled earlier in the game, but he'd also earned the trust of his coach and teammates throughout the regular season. His 2,036 yards of total offense accounted for a third of his team's total. He took another hand-off and picked up 5 yards and a first down, but he failed to get out of bounds.

They took a time-out, then followed it with another completion to the wide receiver for a 17-yard gain. But he, too, failed to get out of bounds. With the ball on the defense's 48 and the clock running, the halfback again circled out of the backfield for a 13-yard catch-and-run to the 35. It was a repeat of the drive's first play. Another 10 yards would put them in field-goal range.

The quarterback badly overthrew an open receiver on the eighth play of the drive. He looked to the sideline for the next play. As he did, he started leaning to one side, rolling his finger in a circle, and pointing at himself. The coach was confused. He didn't know what his quarterback was trying to communicate. Neither did the quarterback. He'd nearly blacked out just before the last play and was struggling to regain his composure. They were running a no-huddle offense, and the need to scream instructions and the snap count to his teammates, as well as the excitement of the moment, had depleted his oxygen.

His focus returned, and he completed his next pass to the half-back. The drive was still on, except for the penalty flag on the ground. The center, playing the last game of his Pro Bowl career, had been too eager to get downfield and throw a block. The official said he'd crossed the line of scrimmage early and flagged him as an ineligible receiver downfield. What had been first-and-ten at the 35 was now second-and-twenty at the 45. Was it a drive-killing mistake or just another obstacle to overcome?

A minute and twenty-two seconds remained in their season as the quarterback came under center. *Get the ball to somebody who can keep it moving forward.*

The ball was snapped for the ninth play of the drive, and the quarterback took his drop, scanning the field and looking for an open receiver. He found him at the 33 where the wide receiver gathered in his third reception of the drive, broke a tackle, and made it to the 18. First-and-ten. At the snap, the tight end again took the linebacker with him, clearing a space for the back to circle underneath. It was the third time in the drive they had run the play, and it picked up another 8 yards. Great field position. Exactly where they wanted to be. It would be an easy field goal from there, just like in the first half. Yeah, the first half, when the center had disrupted the timing of the holder by firing the snap into his leg instead of his open hands.

A time-out was called to discuss the situation—second down, ball on the 10, thirty-nine seconds and one time-out remaining. There was time for two plays before a field-goal attempt.

Red Right Tight-F Left-20 HB Curl X-Up was the first play.

Just before settling under the center, the quarterback glanced over his shoulder. It was a habit he had formed to make sure the backs were lined up correctly. They weren't. He knew he was in trouble if the defense blitzed from his right. But he didn't want to burn the final time-out. They might need it to get the field-goal team onto the field. It could have been a distraction. Instead, he crouched behind the center and began the count.

The quarterback took the snap and the halfback, once again the primary receiver on the play, looped out of the backfield to the right. The defense had him covered this time. Unfazed, the quarterback continued his progressions and looked to his left for his second choice, a man who had not caught a single pass in the game. Didn't matter. They had practiced this so many times.

As the receiver split the seam in the Cincinnati Bengals' zone, quarterback Joe Montana stepped and threw "probably the best pass I've ever thrown," a Super Bowl–winning touchdown to John Taylor.

"Actually this drive is still pretty fresh in my memory," Montana reflected years later. "Mostly because what we did in the two-minute offense...were all plays we had run a million times in practice, every day, every week, usually from day one in training camp. They were all plays that everyone knew. We could have run them in our sleep."

THE SEXUAL DRIVE IN MARRIAGE

Plays that everyone knows. Practiced to the point of becoming second nature. I've studied marriage. And I've studied my wife. I know what it takes to succeed in our marriage. I've run the plays. I've run them in practice. I've run them in the game. I know what I'm doing. At least I know what I'm supposed to be doing.

But sometimes I get distracted. I get busy. I get complacent. And there are times when I choose the easy way out instead of doing the work of relationship. I don't pay attention to Tari as I know I should. Unfortunately, most of the time I don't even realize it until I begin to feel sexually frustrated. When I begin to feel that way, I stop and look back at how I've been interacting with her. And I can almost always see that I haven't been paying attention to the fundamentals. We have a strong marriage, but it won't stay that way unless both of us continue to work at it.

One of the most important ways we work at it is to "speak" each other's love language. In his book *The Five Love Languages,* Gary Chapman identifies five different ways people express and receive love: (1) acts of service, (2) words of affirmation, (3) gifts, (4) time together, and (5) touch. Each one of us, men and women, has one or two of these "languages" that communicate love to us more clearly and effectively than the others. When someone "speaks" them, we feel loved. When we don't "hear" them, we don't feel loved. We may feel valued, maybe even acknowledge in our minds that the person loves us, but we don't feel love at the deep, soul level.

If your primary love language is acts of service, then you will feel most loved when your spouse does things for you. If you feel most loved when your partner says positive things to you, then words of affirmation is your language. Time together just means that you most enjoy your mate's focused attention. You could be sharing an activity or a conversation, but you're doing it together, and the relationship is the focus. If touch is your language, simple physical contact most clearly says, "I love you." And though sex may be a part of this, the vast majority of touches will be nonsexual.

Gifts can be a tricky one. We might be intimidated because we think that gifts have to be big, expensive, or hit the center of the just-the-right-gift bull's-eye every time. They don't have to be any of those, but they do have to show that you know your wife and what's important to her. That shows that you're thinking of her. It also shows you're purposeful enough about the relationship to communicate in this way. And, like all the other languages, they do have to be consistently expressed.

There are a couple of things you should know about love languages. First, we're more likely to express love for our wives in our own language. Like most couples, my wife's is different from mine.

Neither one of us naturally "speaks" the other's language. However, we learned that if we were going to have a successful marriage, we needed to learn some new languages.

I know that my inclination to do things for Tari is not the way to make her feel really loved. She is grateful when I do things for her. But acts of service are my love language, not hers. Conversely, I appreciate when she tells me how much she loves me and touches me. But words of affirmation and physical touch are her languages. They don't really make me feel as loved as acts of service.

The second thing is that we don't have to understand why our wives have the languages they do. It doesn't have to make sense to us, and ours don't have to make sense to them. But we must understand that it is important. Whether we get it or not, we have to do it.

Learning about love languages was a turning point in our relationship. But just because we know about them doesn't mean we always execute. If we're not intentional about it, we can slip. Most often the first indicator is when I express love in my language instead of Tari's. If the trend continues, I find myself making little excuses for not being attentive. I promise myself that I'll get back on track, just as soon as…whatever is the excuse of the moment.

Sometimes there are legitimate reasons, but more often it's a matter of trying to justify my lack of focus and effort. I've found that if I don't make the effort to consciously speak her language, then my focus drifts to what's easy for me. And what's easy for me is not the way to create the right relational environment for a consistent sex life.

Another way we work at it is to nurture our fondness and admiration for each other. It's one of the principles John Gottman and Nan Silver discuss in *The Seven Principles for Making Marriage Work*. They call them "two of the most crucial elements in a rewarding and long-lasting romance." It's the habit of choosing to think about the positive qualities of your spouse. It's the same spirit as Philippians 4:8, which encourages us to dwell on things that are "admirable...excellent or praiseworthy."

As time goes by, conflicts and disappointments occur. And the ease and excitement of early love is replaced by the work of building a mature love. You've noticed, right? It can be easier to focus on what's wrong with your spouse rather than on what's right. That trend ensures you will not have a satisfying sexual relationship.

Nurturing your fondness and admiration doesn't mean you overlook the issues in your marriage. It does mean managing conflict and refusing to let it overwhelm the positives in your partner and your marriage. Understand that not all conflicts will be resolved. But also understand that it is impossible to be either physically intimate or connected in a healthy way if we don't feel accepted, respected, and trusted.

Look for the good, and extend grace while you each continue the process of becoming more like Christ. I've found I'm more likely to see the good when I make the effort to look for it. And when I see it, I need to say it. Out loud. Directly to Tari. Verbally acknowledging my wife's good qualities can be huge, and it's doubly encouraging to her. First, it feels good to receive a compliment. Second, it makes her feel good to hear her husband investing in the relationship. And I've also found it's just as important to me. I need to hear myself say positive things about Tari.

Speaking each other's love languages, managing conflict, choosing to focus on the positives—all contribute to the environment necessary for a mutually satisfying sexual relationship. Quite a list to think about. But if you have to think about them, life will probably win the battle for your attention. There's just too much going on. It's the tyranny of the urgent. That's why it's important to develop those qualities so they become second nature.

Do you think Joe Montana didn't have a lot to think about every time he dropped back to pass? "If you've ever gotten stuck in the median, and it's not very wide, and you feel the cars whizzing by, and you know if you move in one direction or the other you'll get hit—that's about the same thing" is how he once described an NFL pass rush.

The success of the 49ers ensured they would always get the best opponents the league schedule makers could come up with. But even the best of the best couldn't keep Montana from completing 63 percent of the 5,391 passes he attempted in his sixteen-year career. His career passer rating of 92.3 is the second highest of all time. He rallied his team to victory thirty-one times after they trailed or were tied in the fourth quarter. He led his team to four Super Bowls and won all four. He earned MVP honors in three. His quarterback rating in the championship games was 127.8.

Pressure? I think so. Distractions? You bet. Worthy opponents?

The very best. But only one other starting Super Bowl quarterback has earned four rings. I'd say he got the job done. Montana is done as a player. His playing days are over, but our playing days aren't. We're still in the game. We're never done as husbands.

Another way that we work at it is to stay connected. Before we were married, we thought it would be easy for a married couple to do. You probably did too. Now we know it's not. Like most people, our lives move pretty fast. The demands of our jobs, the energy required by our ministry involvements, making time to stay connected with friends—all compete for our emotional energy. We see the same things in the lives of our friends. Oh, and don't forget the investment you're making in the lives of your children.

Because we see each other every day, it can be easy to fall into a roommate-type relationship. We still love each other. We're considerate. And we're vaguely aware of what's going on in each other's lives. But our connection is becoming weaker, not stronger.

True connection requires more than vague awareness. It's Gottman's concept of Love Maps that we discussed in chapter 7. Couples that don't make it a priority to stay in touch with each other's lives will be challenged to maintain the connectedness necessary for a long-term, mutually satisfying physical relationship. They will also be challenged to maintain any kind of vitality in the marriage.

Love languages, managing conflict, nurturing our fondness and admiration, staying connected—all these things *and more* are required if you want to experience satisfying sex. How about defending the harmony of our relationships from the distractions of the world around us and the demands of self-centeredness? How about making scheduling choices so that intimate connection is a priority rather than an afterthought? How about striving to understand God's design for sex as an intensely unifying and pleasurable part of marriage? How about… The list could go on and on. But we should be getting better and better.

" 'The Drive' was the culmination and embodiment of not only ten years of work with the San Francisco 49ers, but of a lifetime of study and refinement," says Walsh. "Each player knew his assignment and carried it out. There was no panic, no hesitation. The players knew they had prepared for this moment and that they possessed the abilities and means to finish the job."

Sex isn't an isolated event in marriage. It occurs within the overall context of the relationship. Each spouse contributes to that context by being open, honest, accepting, and loving, or by being isolated, deceptive, conditional, and self-serving. If we're frustrated with our sexual relationship, we can reasonably assume that one or more aspects of the marriage is frustrating for our wives. We can complain, demand, or attempt to manipulate a response. Or we can take a step back. We can ask ourselves if we're playing a fundamentally sound game. The ultimate goal isn't a great sexual relationship but a great marriage. However, if we take the steps to build a great marriage, we'll have a satisfying sexual relationship.

Because so much goes into a couple's sexual relationship, it may be the truest test of what's really going on in the marriage. All of us want to consistently connect sexually with our wives. I do. But I know that first I must be a student of my wife. And I must be willing to do the small, daily things that create the necessary environment. If we succumb to the pressures and distractions of life and fail to do those things, we will fail in achieving a sexually satisfying marriage.

But what exactly is a sexually satisfying marriage?

You'll need to talk about that as a couple. The stronger your trust and confidence in each other grows and the more firmly established the "serve one another in love" trend is, the easier it will be for you to discuss your sexual relationship. When your marriage is on a solid foundation, you are free to explore the adventure of your sexuality. You can engage in an honest, respectful, and extremely vulnerable discussion about what you like to do, what you don't like to do, and when, where, and how often you like to do it.

That kind of talk might sound like it's from another planet to a lot of us. That's because no area of our lives may be more subject to the influence of our culture and its distortions than sex. It's not just that today we live in a sex-oriented society that continually bombards us with sexual images and references. It's also true that many of our ideas about sex were shaped when we were much younger. The television shows and movies we watched, the books and magazines we read, and the influence of a similarly naive and vulnerable peer group all shaped our sexuality. Perhaps there even were adults who abused us or encouraged us to believe that sexual experience was a fast track to adulthood.

For many of us, those ideas made it to our hearts and minds before we had a biblical perspective on God's gift of sexual intimacy. It should be encouraging to know that God wants husbands and wives to have a blast sexually. But getting there may require cleanup work as we investigate how far we have strayed from the biblical ideal.

Difficult discussion to have? Probably so for most of us. But it shouldn't be. And if we're developing the qualities necessary for a Super Bowl marriage, it won't be. Sex really is where it all comes together.

Successful spouses never stop working on the fundamentals. Love languages, conflict management, love maps, serving one another in love—successful spouses don't leave "all that stuff behind" in their dating relationship or even the first year of marriage. And they don't do those things just when they feel like it or when it is convenient. They become poised, accomplished veterans of the marriage game. And they enjoy the benefits of true sexual intimacy.

The Extra Point

You look up at the clock—3:10 left with the ball at your own 8-yard line. You need the touchdown. Your teammates are heading onto the field to await you. Bill Walsh gives you the play, pats you on the back, and sends you out to battle. Three steps onto the field you stop, come back, and ask, "What was the play again?"

Surprised, he repeats it and asks, "You okay?"

"Yeah, I'm okay. Who am I looking for again? I know we've been over this, but I've forgotten," you respond.

"What's going on? Are you in the game or not?" the coach asks.

"Yeah, yeah. I just have a lot on my mind: different business deals, a couple of important deadlines next week, things coming up with the kids. I've been thinking more about my folks, too. They can't get around like they used to. I'll be okay. Look, we have a lot of time. We've done this before. A field goal will tie it; that's good enough. We'll be okay. We'll win in overtime if we have to. Who am I looking for again?"

"Come on. We've practiced this hundreds of times. We've been here before. Focus on the fundamentals. Just keep the ball moving forward."

———

What love language makes your wife feel most loved? What is yours?

Love languages, conflict management, nurturing your fondness and admiration for each other, making a point to stay connected—how are you doing in your relationship fundamentals?

Is your marriage at a point where you could have an honest, respectful, loving discussion with your wife about your sexual relationship?

outside the box

Two kinds of football players ain't worth a _____.
One that never does what he's told and
the other that does nothing but what he's told.

—Bum Phillips

It was a stumbling, bumbling, fumbling performance worthy of The Three Stooges. These three were no stooges, however.

The tight end had been an academic all-American at Notre Dame. In high school he'd been an all-state linebacker but then spent his first three years in South Bend as an offensive lineman. As a senior he had been moved to the tight-end position. This was a guy who knew how to adapt.

The quarterback had been described by San Francisco's Bill Walsh as "a wonderful clutch performer with great instincts. Other than Joe [Montana], he was the best come-from-behind quarterback I've ever seen."

The running back was a blue-collar player. Though never a star, his whatever-it-takes attitude was the key to a thirteen-year NFL career. He knew what his role was. In 1975 his role was scoring touchdowns, which he did more efficiently than anyone else in the conference. He tied O. J. Simpson for the conference lead with sixteen rushing touchdowns. Remarkably, he did in 187 attempts what it took Simpson 329 to accomplish.

The quarterback, the running back, and the tight end. Three teammates sharing a simple goal in this game: score a touchdown and convert the extra point, or start the season 0-2. They knew that no Super Bowl team had ever started the season 0-2. Even though the NFL was in its inaugural sixteen-game season, 0-2 was not where they wanted to be, especially if both losses were to AFC Western Division rivals.

No question about it, they had Super Bowl potential. Two years before, they had suffered only one loss on their way to a 32–14 hammering of the Minnesota Vikings in the Super Bowl. And they had followed that up with an 11-3 season in which they never suffered back-to-back defeats.

The goal was simple. Reaching it, however, would not be easy. The team had just taken over the ball at their own 19-yard line. They had all three time-outs left, but only one minute and seventeen seconds remained in the game. In the first fifty-nine minutes of this showdown for California bragging rights, they had scored only two touchdowns in twelve possessions. They had given up three and trailed 20–14. The quarterback had been sacked three times and generally harassed all afternoon. Of the twenty-eight passes he had thrown, only twelve had been completed to his own teammates. The defense had snagged three interceptions. Not a great afternoon's work.

One last shot.

The quarterback began his last-ditch attempt with his seventeenth incompletion but followed that with three straight completions. They took their second time-out after the third catch, a 27-yard strike to the opponent's 33. After another incompletion, the quarterback was on target again, picking up another 13 to the 14-yard line, where they stopped the clock with their last time-out. Time remained for two plays, maybe three. Better be quick, though.

The quarterback overthrew a wide receiver in the back of the end zone. The ball was still on the 14, but only ten seconds remained. The official set the ball, and the offense came to the line for what would likely be their last chance. At the snap an outside linebacker took off on a blitz. The defense had successfully pressured the quarterback all day. The linebacker wasn't going to let the passer get set and wait for a receiver to get open.

The play was supposed to develop quickly. When the linebacker shot across the line, the running back cut him at the knees, hoping to occupy him long enough for the quarterback to find an open man. The receivers were covered, however. After the linebacker untangled himself from the falling running back, he began lunging, scrambling, grasping for the quarterback, who was backpedaling while circling away from the rush and scanning the end zone. He hoped to find his favorite target, the tight end, who was dragging across the middle. The play had worked earlier in the game. Not this time, however.

The running back jumped to his feet, just in time to see the linebacker finally reach the quarterback, pinning his left arm and the ball to his leg for the apparent game-ending sack at the 24. The quarterback had taken too much time in his desperate back-pedal. There was no time for another play, and the back knew the game was over. Then he noticed the ball rolling on the ground.

A brief but relevant aside: NFL footballs are made by Wilson Sporting Goods. They must be 11–11¼ inches at the long axis, have a long circumference of 28–28½ inches, a short circumference of 21–21¼ inches, and weigh 14–15 ounces when inflated to the pre-scribed pressure of 12½–13½ pounds. The home team is responsible for having twenty-four balls ready for game use. Another twelve are set aside solely for use in kicking situations. That's all in the rule book.

A football is an aerodynamic marvel when thrown. A tightly spiraling pass that settles into the hands of a receiver in full stride is a beautiful play to watch. A fumble is an altogether different matter. When dropped, a football becomes a comic adventure and is virtually guaranteed to do the unexpected. And the unexpected can quickly become slapstick comedy when players from both teams hold a human demolition derby as they attempt to knock each other away and corral the fumbled ball.

Now back to our game. Was this ball on a wobbly roll on the ground a fumble or futile pass? Nobody knew for sure. The whistle hadn't blown, so the chase was on.

The running back was the first to get near the ball. But as he did, he was hit from behind. He could have recovered the fumble.

Fall on it—that's what he had always been coached to do, but he would not have accomplished the desired result. He was getting tackled before he even had possession of the ball.

"You bet I batted it toward the goal line," he later admitted. "If I'd picked it up, I'd never have scored. It was the logical thing to do."

As it rolled to the 5-yard line, the tight end swooped in. He was unable to control it, so he, too, batted the ball. As he stumbled toward the goal line, he began to surround the ball with his falling body. Hands, elbows, knees, anything he could do to minimize the bouncing. When he finally guided it across the goal line, he fell on it.

The coach appeared more hopeful than confident as he lumbered toward the official. He wasn't even sure it would count. He weakly raised his arms, as if to say, "Now that's a touchdown, right?"

He was right. It was a touchdown. The extra point that followed gave his team a 21–20 victory.

When the owners met during the following off-season, some rule changes were discussed. One change that was accepted: on fourth down or in the last two minutes of either half, a fumble could only be advanced by the player who originally fumbled the ball. No more "holy rollers." That was of no consolation to the San Diego Chargers whose last-second, 21–20 loss to the Oakland Raiders was critical in their failure to make the playoffs in 1978. You won't find this sort of play in any team's playbook, but the resourcefulness of the fumbling Kenny Stabler, the bumbling Pete Banaszak, and the stumbling Dave Casper won the game.

GETTING CREATIVE TO WIN THE MARRIAGE GAME

What does it take to win the marriage game?

A consistent, disciplined approach is essential. Developing the discipline to consistently speak each other's love languages is an important part of a successful marriage. We should identify ways to express our love and commitment to our wives in ways they intuitively feel and understand that love. We must manage conflict, also. We have to work to respectfully resolve the issues that can be resolved. And we must patiently learn to work with our differences, the things about each other that may never change.

It's helpful to focus on the things that are good about our wives. Our positive feelings can be overwhelmed if we focus on the bad. We have to take the steps to stay connected. Stay in touch with her life, and let her know what's going on in yours.

It's a lot to remember. That's why we keep working at it until it becomes second nature. It's a way of life, not a thought process. But even then, you may need a little more. Once in a while, you might need something a little special. It could mean the difference between winning and losing.

You couldn't argue with Jim's results. He usually accomplished what he set out to do. He had learned how to win. No longer a fresh rookie, his game had changed a lot over the years. The biggest difference? His motives. He was older and wiser, a little less concerned about himself and a lot more concerned about his teammate: Sheri, his wife of twenty-five years.

Jim once picked up Sheri at work to take her to lunch. When they got into the car, Jim had her put on a blindfold so she couldn't see where they were going. A few minutes later she found herself at a local getaway especially designed for romantic interludes. Jim had arranged with Sheri's boss for her to have the afternoon off, and they made the most of their afternoon adventure.

"Maybe early on I had ulterior motives," admits Jim. "You know, get the wife in a good mood, see what happens. Now the relationship is deeper. I think my understanding of things like love languages, forgiveness, serving one another, and God's design for marriage is better. These creative things are motivated by much deeper things."

A disciplined approach is essential, but don't be surprised if you or your wife begins to feel a little complacent. Positive things begin to lose some of their impact when they are repeated with predictable regularity. Once a need is consistently met, we begin to develop the subconscious expectation that it will always be met. Without intending to, we forget that meeting our needs may take a significant effort on the part of our spouses. We might start taking their efforts for granted. And when our most important needs are being met, we might become more aware of other needs that aren't being met.

If that's the case, a principle of behavioral science called random reinforcement may be helpful. Psychologists tell us that variable or random rewards can be far more helpful than known rewards in influencing behavior. Of course, it's not behavior that we're trying to influence. We're trying to influence how our wives feel about the relationship. And we're trying to influence how we feel about the relationship. We're striving to create an environment of love, acceptance, and security. We're reinforcing the value by continuing to invest in it.

But even after we've created that environment, once in a while we need to make a statement. Deliver a message. "Good enough" may not be good enough. We're showing our wives, and ourselves, that expressing love isn't just a box to check off. It's a dynamic process, and we're engaged.

Jim has an attitude of random reinforcement. He is a rarity in that this comes naturally to him. He's always been good at expressing his love for Sheri in creative ways. He never wanted their marriage to lapse into a predictable routine. He recognized the value of making a special effort to do something a little unusual once in a while.

Sheri loves flowers. They have a backyard full of them, and they didn't grow there by accident. She was intentional about planting them. Jim is intentional about what he plants in their relationship as well. He understands that one of the ways he can creatively express his love for Sheri is by sending her flowers.

Sometimes it's for a special occasion. Sometimes it's to say he is sorry. Often it is simply because Jim understands that Sheri loves flowers. It tells her that Jim knows her unique likes. He has paid attention to her. He has learned the things that are important to Sheri so he can express his love in ways that are not only unique but also meaningful to her.

He had a problem: he needed to do creative things to make

Sherry feel cherished. Rather than going through a whole decision-making process of what to do and where to go every time he wanted to do something for her, he developed an easy solution. Jim set up an account with a local florist.

"I have found, over the years, that you need to be intentional about these things. When something romantic is on your mind, whether it's ordering flowers, stopping and picking up a card, or making a phone call, as soon as you think it, do it," advises Jim. "That's the reason for the account. It's easier! Make a phone call and off the flowers go."

It is no less meaningful to Sheri that Jim has a system. She is flattered that it was important enough to him to create the solution, and she feels loved when they arrive.

Jim's creativity is not confined to big expressions. He used to travel every week with his job. He would frequently buy a card or write a quick note and mail it to her. Instead of spending money, he spent a few minutes to communicate to Sheri how he felt. If Sheri has had a particularly stressful day or week, Jim will sometimes come home with candles and encourage her to take a long, relaxing bath. It is another way she knows he is aware of her and what she is going through. Sometimes it's the things we do. Sometimes it's when we do them. The right thing at the right time can make all the difference.

Some say the Raiders got lucky that day. True, there was some luck involved. But they were in a position to win the game when they took over with 1:17 left. They'd already scored 14 points. If they hadn't, Stabler's creativity would have been merely amusing. A goofy, last-second touchdown doesn't do you much good if you're still behind when the clock shows 0:00.

And they were in a position to win with the ball on the Chargers' 14-yard line with only ten seconds left. That would not have been the case if Stabler hadn't completed four passes to move the ball from their own 19. A 24-yard fumble is a once-in-a-career fluke, even if it was an intentional fluke. But a 40- or 50-yard fumble? Not hardly. A single act of creativity will only get you so far. But because the Raiders had scored earlier in the game and executed earlier in that series, they were in a position to win by a single creative impulse. The right thing at the right time.

That's true in marriage, too. About now you might be saying "Yeah, but…"

For example, "Yeah, but…I've never been any good at that kind of thing." Most men aren't naturally good at this kind of thing. That's why you start small. As a matter of fact, you can stay small. You don't have to arrange for your wife to get the afternoon off, pick her up in a limo, and spirit her away to a hotel suite. But try some things. Take a chance on love. After an awkward time or two, it'll get easier.

When you think of something positive about her during the day, pick up the phone and call. Or try writing "I love you" on the bathroom mirror with a dry-erase pen. If you know she's having a tough day or week, pick up a single rose or a simple flower arrangement to give her. If she does something so consistently for you that you both don't even notice anymore, try noticing. Step back from your life. See the things she does. And acknowledge her efforts for you. These are not big things. But they can have big impact, especially if you haven't been doing them.

"Yeah, but…I love her, just in different ways." But are those different ways her ways? The point is not to communicate your love in ways that are easy for you. The point is to communicate your love in ways she understands. And make sure she understands what you're communicating. Doing something special, even if it's small, is like an enormous exclamation point on the statement "I love you!" It's rising above the noise of life and the expectation of what's normal. Most likely, that will stretch you. But my experiences tell me that if I'm not being stretched, I'm atrophying.

"Yeah, but…this just isn't how we live, neither of us." And this is why we're called to be the leaders in our homes. This is leadership that breaks new ground in the relationship. If we start loving our wives creatively, perhaps they will respond with creative expressions of their own. I believe the responsibility is on us husbands when its comes to the direction of the marriage. Either we're serving ourselves and playing it safe or serving our wives and taking some chances to move the relationship ahead.

"Yeah, but…I don't have time for this stuff." C'mon, we have the time. And we always use our time according to our priorities. We do the things that are most important to us—and perhaps the easiest to do. That's how we spend our time. If we followed ourselves around all day and logged how we spent our time, we'd know what's most important to us. We wouldn't necessarily know *why* they're important, but we would know *what* is important.

I'm sure you're like me in that the vast majority of our time is spent productively in worthwhile endeavors. But I'm equally sure that some time is not. I wouldn't have to sacrifice any productive energy to do something different for Tari once a week. Okay, maybe twice one week but nothing the next. Maybe once one month, nothing the next, and twice the next. This is, after all, random. But random does not mean infrequent. Once a year is too random. Consistent. Steady. Just not predictable.

"Yeah, but…what am I going to get out of this?" Okay, we wouldn't outright ask that, but we might think it. Well, for starters we'd be more attuned to our wives and their world. They'd be less of a mystery. We'd be developing an increasingly strong habit of focusing on their needs rather than our own. That's a benefit, because competence is important to most of us. We want to do things well. Being a husband is no different. We'll be the kind of teammates who are growing more confident in our role as husband. Of course, there's always Christlikeness. The fact that we're choosing to serve our wives in love and becoming more like Jesus in the process is a huge benefit.

But if we're really asking, "Yeah, but…what's she going to do for me?" well, that's more like entitlement than love. Here's a crazy thing about love. We don't give to get. We give to give. We give for the well-being of the other. And if the Christian model of love is true, we receive the same measure we give. We will benefit but perhaps not in the ways we expected. That's where faith comes in. Do we have faith in that approach or not?

There was a "Yeah, but…" for Kenny Stabler. Not "Yeah,

but…if a couple of breaks had gone our way," "Yeah, but…the Chargers were a better team today," or "Yeah, but…there's still another fourteen games to go." More like "Yeah, Plan A got us close, *but* I better come up with a Plan B if we're going to win this thing." Of course it was happening so fast that he didn't have time to go through the steps of formal problem solving. Something had to be done, and he did it, regardless of how unorthodox it was. He fumbled the ball forward. It was their only chance to salvage the win. And winning is what they had come to do.

Fumble or incomplete forward pass? Running back Pete Banaszak didn't pause to answer before he shoveled the ball forward. Instincts developed over an athletic lifetime told him "it was the logical thing to do" if he was going to help his team win. Crazy and improbable, sure, but what else could he do?

By the time tight end Dave Casper entered the picture at the 5-yard line, the clock showed 0:00, and the ball was still bouncing unpredictably. It was exactly the kind of game situation that the repetition and routine of practice couldn't prepare him for. Accomplishing the goal demanded a more pragmatic approach.

Most often a husband and wife will build a strong marriage and win the marriage game by methodically executing the plays in the playbook—love languages, forgiveness, serving one another, and more. However, there will be times when the relationship may call for a little creative problem solving. In football and in marriage, winners do what it takes to get the job done. Stabler, Banaszak, and Casper did. So does Jim.

the extra point

"Run the screen pass," you hear on the speaker in your helmet.

You sure? you think as you look to the sideline for a confirming nod. Maybe the two sacks you took have scrambled your head. *We don't run screen passes out of four-wide formations.*

The offensive coordinator knows what you're thinking as you squint at him in concentration. He nods twice, the laminated play sheet still covering his mouth. "The screen," he repeats.

I guess today we're running the screen pass out of a four-wide formation, you think as you turn into the huddle. *The Super Bowl isn't where I expected to try some new things.* The completed pass picks up 14 yards and a first down. Three plays later you run another screen out of a four-wide formation for another first down.

Both times the defenders are as surprised as you. They don't know what to think. They have a lot more to think about now. Now they're reading and reacting. No more jailbreak blitzes. Now you have the time you need as you drive for the first touchdown.

———

Did any of the "Yeah, but…" excuses sound familiar to you as you read this chapter?

Would you be willing to run at least one trick play a month in your marriage?

coming back

*There are a few things a quarterback needs to remember
when his team is behind late in the game. One is that
you need to try and do something, not everything.*

—Joe Montana

It didn't start out as a blowout. As a matter of fact, expectations were high for both teams. The hosts were in the playoffs for the fifth consecutive year. They had won their division the previous four. The last two years they had made it all the way to the Super Bowl. They were accustomed to success. This year they were a wild-card team, however, not a division winner. Getting back to the Super Bowl meant they'd have to win three games, not two.

And they'd have to win the first without their All Pro quarterback, who was on the sideline in street clothes. Starting in his place was the man who once led the greatest comeback in the history of Division I football. But that was eight years earlier. Since that time, he'd thrown only 258 passes as a professional and started only seven games. Their All Pro linebacker didn't dress, either. It was going to be uphill all the way.

The visitors thought this could be their year. It was their sixth straight playoff appearance. Their run-and-shoot quarterback led the AFC in passing by throwing to a trio of Pro Bowl receivers, including the conference's first- and second-leading pass catchers. The running back rushed for 1,226 yards, third highest in the conference, an average of 4.6 yards a carry. In addition to their firepower on offense, the defense sent five players to the Pro Bowl. Most important, they had whipped their hosts 27–3 when the two teams had played their regular season finale only a week before.

The home team kicked off and fourteen plays, 80 yards, and 9:09 later, found themselves trailing 7–0. They came back with a drive of their own to kick a field goal with 1:19 left in the first quarter. It looked as though the game would live up to its high-scoring promise.

Twelve plays later the hosts had yielded another 80-yard touchdown drive, making the score 14–3. The offense held the ball for barely a minute as they went three-and-out and punted. Once again the hosts proved generous. Their opponents needed only 3:43 to run off five plays, the last a 26-yard touchdown pass, to make the score 21–3.

The game threatened to get out of hand. The home team needed to reestablish itself, to at least salvage a measure of respect from the first half. With 4:01 remaining, they took over at their own 29-yard line and began moving the ball. They went for the fourth-and-one at their opponent's 33 and were stuffed with 1:15 left in the half. A discouraging end to a discouraging half.

Getting out of the 18-point hole they had put themselves in would be difficult, but that proved to be the least of their worries. Their opponents took less than a minute to score another touchdown to make the halftime score 28–3. The defense had given up scores on long, grinding drives and alarmingly quick drives. The offense was a virtual no-show. What does a coach say to a team getting dominated in every aspect of the game?

"Whatever happens, you guys have to live with yourselves after today." It was a simple call to manhood.

One play at a time, one play at a time, thought the quarterback. Right. But it wasn't a trite coaching cliché to the quarterback. He knew about comebacks. As a Maryland Terrapin, he'd sat on the sideline nursing a separated shoulder while Bernie Kosar led the Miami Hurricanes to a 31–0 halftime lead. The quarterback started the second half and marched the Terps to scoring drives on six consecutive possessions. Maryland's wild 42–40 victory wasn't certain until a Miami receiver was tackled short of the goal line on a game-tying 2-point conversion attempt with less than a minute to go. It had been a nice footnote to his college career, but this was the NFL. More important, this was the playoffs.

He hadn't played a bad first half, but with their opponents controlling the ball for twenty-one minutes, he simply hadn't played much at all. The offense had only been on the field for less than nine minutes of the game. However, that was long enough for their All Pro running back to aggravate a hip injury. The first back to lead the NFL in combined rushing and receiving yards for four consecutive years would join his All Pro teammates on the sideline as a spectator as the second half started.

The first series would be crucial. They would receive the kickoff to open the second half, so the offense could get started right away. The fans didn't have to wait long for the scoring to resume. On the fourth play from scrimmage, the quarterback's pass slipped through the hands of his tight end and was intercepted by the safety who returned it 58 yards for another touchdown. It was 35–3 with just over twenty-eight minutes to go. Out of hand? This could turn into the kind of thumping not seen in the playoffs since Chicago's 73–0 annihilation of Washington in 1940.

One play at a time. The offense got the ball back at the 50 and ten plays later scored their first touchdown in seven quarters of football against their opponents. At 35–10 you couldn't say the tide had turned, but at least the offense had put some points on the scoreboard.

One play at a time. They had fallen behind as a team, and if they were to get back into the game, they would do so only as a team. The kickoff coverage team recovered the onside kick at the 48. The offensive unit did its part by scoring another touchdown in only four plays, narrowing the gap to 35–17. The defense then rose to the challenge by forcing a three-and-out series. It was the first series that they hadn't given up a score.

One play at a time. The offense took over at their own 41 and, once again, found the end zone in only four plays. They'd scored three touchdowns in four and a half minutes but still trailed 35–24.

One play at a time. The defense forced an interception two plays later. Following two runs and an incompletion, the home team faced a fourth-and-five at their opponent's 18-yard line. A field goal would put points on the board, but they would still have to score at least twice going against the wind in the fourth quarter. The coach elected to go for it.

"It" was not a first down, however. Defying conventional wisdom and choosing not to remember that they had been stopped on a fourth-and-one in the first half, they went for the touchdown. The 18-yard pass for a score justified the coach's gamble. It was 35–31, and two minutes still remained in the third quarter. The two teams traded punts, and the defense took the field again with fourteen minutes and seventeen seconds left in someone's season.

One play at a time. Their opponent's fourteen-play, seven-and-a-half-minute drive finally stalled at the 14, and the kicker trotted onto the field for the 31-yard field-goal attempt just as a gentle drizzle started to fall. A wet ball, a gust of wind, a high snap, and a failed try for a three-pointer. Once again the offense had a chance as they took over at their own 26.

One play at a time. On the seventh play of the drive, the receiver hauled in his third touchdown of the half. They had their first lead of the game with three minutes and eight seconds left in the final period. The defense hadn't given up a score the entire second half, and if they could hold one more time, the team would advance to the next round of the playoffs.

The defense didn't hold but allowed a thirteen-play drive that ended with a field goal with twelve seconds left on the clock to send the game into overtime. The hosts lost the coin toss and kicked off to start the extra period. They intercepted the ball three plays later and had excellent field position at the 20.

One play at a time. Two runs picked up 5 yards and positioned the ball perfectly at the 15. The coach sent in his kicker. With only 3:02 gone in the overtime period, Steve Christie's kick was true. Frank Reich, the little-used understudy to Buffalo's Jim Kelly, had led the Bills to a 41–38 win over the Houston Oilers, completing the greatest comeback in NFL history.

COMING BACK FROM A MARRIAGE BLOWOUT

You don't see many teams come back from 32-point deficits. That's a pretty deep hole. But deep holes and dramatic comebacks aren't limited to the NFL.

A deep hole is exactly what Robert had dug for himself. But it wasn't until his ninth year of marriage that he could admit how deep that hole was. That was when he confessed to his wife that he had been struggling with a sexual addiction for twenty years. He had grown up in a home with a great deal of tension between his mom and dad. His dad hadn't learned how to love and care for his wife. She felt neglected and responded with perfectly timed snide remarks.

She knew how to get under his skin and did so regularly. He neglected her; she picked at him. She picked at him; he neglected her. It was a well-developed pattern.

Robert felt the constant tension at home. As a ten-year-old, his hand began to shake in response to the stress. At thirteen, he discovered one of his dad's pornographic magazines. Shortly after that discovery he came across his sixteen-year-old brother's magazines. He had found the relief he needed from the stress. It was the same relief his dad had found. The adrenaline rush of the pictures, the numbing pleasure of masturbation: he had his escape.

He dated girls in high school, but his natural shyness and sensitivity were compounded by insecurity. His insecurity was exacerbated by his steadily strengthening pornography habit. He hadn't had a significant relationship, and his insecurity grew. He was developing a pattern of responding sexually to the stress in his life.

Robert was falling further behind in the relationship game. Without making the choice or even realizing what was going on, Robert had grown up seeing an unhealthy marriage. It was his standard. He hadn't learned how a man and woman could relate to each other in positive, healthy ways. He never had a successful relationship with a woman through high school or college.

At twenty-two, Robert met Debbie, then nineteen, and they started to date. One year after meeting they moved in together. One year later, possessing no relationship skills and crippled by a reliance on pornography, Robert asked Debbie to marry him. She said yes.

In the late '80s, Robert's addiction took a turn. It was part of the typical progression of an addict. With the growing popularity of VCRs, Robert could now rent pornographic videos. The images were no longer frozen in photographs on pages. There was action, but as with any addict, what once thrilled eventually became routine. It's called tolerance, and Robert found he needed more images and different experiences. The next step in Robert's descent was visiting "modeling studios," where he would masturbate while watching a woman.

Robert's life hadn't started out as a relationship blowout. It became one. He grew up in an unhealthy home. He found a way to relieve the stress he felt. Pornography and masturbation became a response, then a habit. Robert knew how to deal with the stress he felt as an adult: the same way he had learned how to deal with stress as a child.

Age didn't change the pattern. In fact, as he grew older, the pattern caused Robert to become increasingly insecure. Stress led to acting out, which led to shame. That caused more stress, which led to… You get the point. It's a classic cycle. As a result, his marriage had fallen way behind. His secrecy and dependency ensured he would never have the connectedness that both he and Debbie needed. It's the same with any addiction or compulsive behavior. It's tough to develop the know-and-be-known intimacy we were created for when we're keeping a can't-be-found-out secret.

"One of the worst consequences of the addiction is the addict's isolation," says Dr. Patrick Carnes, author of *Out of the Shadows* and

In the Shadows of the Net. If there was going to be a comeback in Robert's life and marriage, it was going to be tough. And it was going to take time.

Frank Reich didn't throw one pass that brought the Bills back from a 32-point deficit. One play at a time, the Bills team started executing better. A completion here, a run there—next thing you know, Kenneth Davis, Thurman Thomas's replacement, scored from one yard out. Special teams came through with a big play. Reich led a four-play drive and tossed a 38-yarder for another score. The defense held. The offense scored. The defense held again, and the offense scored again. The Bills simply started doing the things that successful teams do.

One play at a time. Robert started doing things that successful husbands do. First, he admitted his self-centeredness was destroying his life and marriage. An honest addict has an advantage over many men: he can admit how destructive his pattern of behavior is. Robert did. At this point he knew it was wrong. He knew it was destroying his life and his marriage. And he knew it would destroy the lives of his children. He also knew he couldn't control it. By definition, an addict is someone whose life has become unmanageable.

He also had the advantage of beginning recovery before the Internet became the vehicle for sex that it is today. *Cybersex: The Dark Side of the Force* talks about the Internet being turbocharged by the "Triple A Engine" of *accessibility* (available twenty-four hours a day), *affordability* (competitively priced or even free), and *anonymity* (the privacy of whoever and whatever you want, wherever you can be alone). Whether it's graphic visuals or chat rooms, sex on the Internet is powerfully addictive.

"The addict substitutes a sick [unhealthy] relationship to an event or process for a healthy relationship to others," says Dr. Patrick Carnes. Being controlled by a distorted use of sex was an "advantage" because few reasonable people would argue that it was helping him or his marriage. But sex is just one of the many ways people deal with the cluster of insecurity, fear of abandonment, and shame that drives addictive behaviors. Dependence on drugs and alcohol? Hard to make a case for their being beneficial to true connection and personal development.

But our culture is filled with numerous addictions that substitute the *A* of anonymity with the *A* of acceptability. An unhealthy relationship with food helps many people handle the stresses of their lives. Our well-documented overweight society testifies to that, but it doesn't stop us from overeating.

Some people are controlled by spending. They feel compelled to acquire things. Something about spending feels pleasurable to them. And it may not be big things. Or needed things. Often it's a matter of making up for stress, insecurity, or a relationship void they feel but don't know how to address. When a husband or wife spends like this, the interest charges on credit-card debt can dig a financial hole that may take years to escape. But we often admire people who have a lot of stuff or the right stuff.

Some people are driven by an unhealthy need to perform, an

addiction that most often is expressed in their approach to work. Work often provides the objective measure of accomplishment that marriage does not. There are no illusions about success or failure, and the dynamics are often easier to understand. People don't come face to face with their self-centeredness at work the same way, if at all, as they do at home.

Work and its financial rewards, eating, and sexual intimacy are all intended to be positive, life-enhancing experiences. Excellence in the marketplace should be a matter of stewardship for all Christians. Eating is not only a legitimately pleasurable activity, but it is also a common way to experience community with others. Sex is a gift from God meant to bring pleasure and unity to a couple's marriage. We should be thankful for all these things. They were meant to be enjoyed. But our insecurities can easily twist these God-given desires into self-serving and relationship-disrupting behaviors. Though I have been using the word *addiction,* a desire doesn't have to progress to the level of unmanageable to be harmful. It's easy to develop an unhealthy reliance on work, performance, spending, food, and more. And the more we rely on them for our sense of worth or for escape from life's stresses, the further behind we'll fall in our marriages.

One play at a time. Robert's comeback began when he admitted to Debbie that he had a problem. Though concerned, she was wise enough not to take it personally. Robert's patterns of handling stress in his life were well established before they met. She was also wise enough to know it was bigger than the two of them. They sought help. The counselor they saw, who was part of Debbie's insurance plan, was of little help. That didn't stop them. It only meant they had to look somewhere else for a solution. A new pattern of honestly addressing the problem was being established. Honesty was critical, because people who are sexually addicted or compulsive are notoriously skilled deceivers.

One play at a time. The second step Robert took was to accept Christ. The grip of his addiction convinced him of his sin, but accepting Christ alone wasn't enough to break the patterns of twenty years. He started attending a Journey Towards Wholeness group where he met an accountability partner to walk with him. Now he had somebody with whom he could share his struggle. More important, it was someone who knew the ins and outs of sexual addiction. Someone who knew what Robert was up against. Someone who could both love him and challenge him. Once he had the power of Christ and the loving accountability of a friend, he could face his responsibilities. He could focus on the needs of Debbie and their children rather than himself.

One play at a time. He joined a group at his church called Journeymen. The men met regularly and discussed true biblical manhood, including the role of men as husbands and fathers. It was information all men should get but many of us don't. Robert learned about things like love languages. Debbie found herself responding to his efforts. She was drawn to the man who was emerging in the role of her husband.

Patience and perseverance are the keys. Habits learned in childhood, reinforced in the teen years, and solidified as adults are not easily broken. New patterns of thought and behavior have to replace the old patterns. It's a process that takes honest confession, a commitment to the process of recovery, determined effort, firm and loving encouragement and support, and time. The new patterns need to be constantly repeated and reinforced. They don't happen quickly.

Comebacks are rarely a line of recovery going straight up. There are frequently disappointments and setbacks. A key to sustaining any comeback is how a team recovers when there are disappointments. Teams need minicomebacks within the comeback.

The Bills were already hurt by the absence of All Pros Jim Kelly and Cornelius Bennett. They were dealt what could have been a crippling blow when Thurman Thomas, their All Pro running back, reinjured his hip in the first half. Instead, Kenneth Davis rose to the challenge.

When the Bills were still trailing 35–17, a 40-yard completion to the Oilers' 1-yard line was called back for illegal procedure. That can take the wind out of a team's sails. It didn't, however. Rather than dwell on what went wrong, Bills' quarterback Frank Reich attacked the problem, one play at a time. He followed the penalty with an 18-yard completion and then a 26-yarder for a touchdown to Andre Reed.

In the fourth quarter, linebacker Carlton Bailey thwarted a Houston drive by picking off a Warren Moon pass at the Buffalo 25. Bruce Smith was flagged for a 15-yard roughing-the-passer penalty, however, nullifying the interception and giving the Oilers an automatic first down. Six plays later, the snap on the field-goal attempt slipped through the hands of Houston's holder as they attempted a 32-yarder. Buffalo had dodged another bullet.

Robert had some lapses early in his recovery process. He would respond to stress in his life by fantasy and masturbation. Rather than quit on the recovery process or deny his relapse, he would confess to his accountability partners and then move on. He learned to focus on what was ahead of him, not what was behind. "Forgetting what is behind and straining toward what is ahead" (Philippians 3:13), Robert followed the apostle Paul's advice and pressed on.

Setbacks are not fatal. Successful players on a football team or on a marriage team learn from their mistakes, recommit, and move on. The ones who don't, fall further and further behind.

Robert came back from a deficit most men never do, but he knows he will never be "recovered." His recovery is an ongoing process, not a single event. He is still vigilant about how the stresses of life affect him. He knows what his triggers are. He knows that when he is very tired or hungry, he will begin to focus on himself. He knows he is susceptible to falling into old behavior patterns at those times.

However, stress at work is the most powerful trigger. He is especially vigilant when he is under a lot of stress at work. He knows he can begin to focus on the discomfort he is feeling and the response habits he used to have. He knows a billboard he passes on the highway might be enough to plant a seed and accelerate his self-centeredness. He also knows enough to work the program. He calls

an accountability partner, someone who cares about his life, someone with whom he has taken the time to develop a relationship. No
judgments, just someone to speak the truth to him and get him
back on track.

At 35–3 the game threatened to become the biggest playoff
blowout in the Super Bowl era. Instead, the Bills' 41–38 win was
the greatest comeback. Whatever the end, blowout or comeback,
the means would have been the same: one play at a time.

The playoffs are like marriage. They can bring out the best or
the worst in a person. Over time, the true person will be exposed,
one way or another. A marriage team is only as strong as its weakest
member. And a team member is only as strong as his or her ability
to handle the toughest challenge.

the extra point

It could be your last half of football for a few months. You were
everybody's preseason Super Bowl favorite. But the high hopes of
August gave way to the grim realities of a season of injuries and sub-
par performances. You backed into the playoffs via a tiebreaker.
Down by seventeen at the start of the second half, Bruce Smith
pulls you aside. He's been playing with cracked ribs.

"We'll hold 'em," he assures you. "One play at a time. Count
on us. You guys have to put some points on the board. This is no
way to end this season."

"I don't know. You guys have given up twenty already. You

aren't playing well. And we've only scored a field goal. Three points in one half. We stink."

"Look, one play at a time," he continues. "We'll do our job. Do yours. You don't have to score three touchdowns on the next series. Just move the ball. One play at a time we'll get back into this thing."

———

Finances. Confidence in each other. Mutual respect. Your sexual relationship. Is there a behavior or thought pattern that's causing you to fall behind in your marriage?

Taking it one step at a time, what can you do today to begin the comeback to instill confidence in your teammate about your commitment and the direction of the relationship?

keeping your Head in the game

*I had to realize every mistake I made was a lesson.
Instead of thinking about how many times I had been
beaten, I decided to think about how many
lessons I had learned.*

—MEL BLOUNT

The day would come when the receiver would set an NFL record with twenty receptions in a single game. This was not that day, however. This day was a different kind of memorable.

The receiver's team had won their division in twelve of the last sixteen years, a stretch that included five Super Bowl wins. They were a ruling NFL dynasty. The crown was slipping, however. For the second time in three years, they were a wild-card team, a dynasty on the downside.

Their playoff run couldn't have had a worse beginning.

On the game's third play from scrimmage, the quarterback ducked under the blitzing safety and fired a perfect strike to the receiver as he slanted toward the middle. He gathered the ball in for a first down and headed upfield. A defensive back, pursuing from behind, poked the ball away. The defense recovered the fumble.

The receiver watched from the sideline with the rest of the offense as their opponents scored first, concluding a nine-play drive with a 22-yard field goal. Everyone makes mistakes, but this one had obvious consequences.

Since being drafted out of Tennessee–Chattanooga in the third round in 1996, the receiver had steadily developed into one of the league's premier wideouts. He caught thirty-five passes, four for touchdowns, in his rookie season. He avoided the sophomore jinx with a sixty-catch, eight-touchdown year in his second season. Though his reception total increased only to sixty-seven in 1998, his touchdowns nearly doubled, jumping to fourteen. He was emerging as an impact player.

It surprised nobody that the receiver's team was in the playoffs. They had qualified for postseason play in fifteen of the last seventeen years. No surprise about their opponents, either. They had earned a spot in the playoffs for the last five years and had played in the last two Super Bowls. It had been seven years since at least one of these teams wasn't playing in the NFC championship game.

An additional pattern had emerged, however. These two teams were opposing each other in the playoffs for the fourth consecutive year. In the previous three meetings, the receiver's team had allowed their opponents to score first. They had lost all three. They had wanted to avoid mistakes and establish early momentum. Instead, they had committed the turnover, and the other team had drawn first blood.

In the third quarter the receiver's team had driven to their opponent's 8-yard line. On second down his fake to the post was a thing of deceptive beauty. He was as open as a man can be as he cut toward the corner of the end zone. The quarterback was right on the money with a perfectly timed, perfectly thrown touch pass. Right into the glare of the sun as it turned out. The blinded receiver barely touched the ball before it fell incomplete, his second drop of the day. A teammate caught the next pass for a touchdown.

Later in that same quarter the receiver's team faced a second-and-seven. Once again the quarterback took the snap, retreated three quick steps, and threw. The wide receiver had come off the line hard, driving the defender back before breaking off the pattern and curling back. Once again he was open. Once again he dropped the ball.

"I don't think I've ever seen [him] play as poorly as he is today," said the announcer. "He is [the quarterback's] go-to guy."

Perhaps no failure is more apparent than a mishandled pass, whether dropped or fumbled. Not only is it a failed play, it can undermine a player's and team's confidence. An offensive line can block flawlessly. A quarterback can throw a perfectly timed, perfectly accurate spiral. And a receiver can run a deceptively precise pattern. But if he doesn't catch the ball, the results are the same as if the whole team had performed poorly. An opportunity is squandered, and everyone knows it.

The game had been as dramatic as their previous three had been disappointing. Midway through the fourth quarter there had already been three lead changes. With only six minutes and thirteen seconds remaining, the receiver's team kicked a field goal to take a 23–20 lead, breaking the fourth tie of the game.

The defense again rose to the occasion after the kickoff by immediately intercepting a pass at their opponent's 40-yard line. They'd seized control. Only five minutes and fifty-three seconds remained. Run some time off the clock. Kill it altogether if possible. Another 15 yards and they'd be in position for a field goal that would create a 6-point cushion. A touchdown would almost certainly put an end to their playoff frustration.

After two runs, the receiver's team was still at the 40, 10 yards from the first down with four minutes and thirty-one seconds left. A first down would make a huge difference. Someone had to step up.

Discouraged? The receiver had dropped three passes and fumbled away another. Time after time after time he had let his teammates down. Embarrassed? In addition to his teammates, coaches, opponents, and more than sixty-six thousand people in the stadium, a national television audience had witnessed his ineptitude. There was no place to hide and no excuse to offer. He simply had not done his job, and his team was fortunate to be ahead.

Third-and-ten. The receiver was in the slot on the left, a step off the line with a teammate split farther out. At the snap of the ball they both took off. The play developed exactly as it had been drawn in the playbook. The cornerback went deep with the wideout. The safety, playing the inside, couldn't cover the slot receiver on an out pattern.

The quarterback patted the ball twice as he stood in the pocket and waited until just before the cut. The receiver had to make sure he made his break beyond the first-down marker. At the 30, he planted his inside foot. The quarterback realized that the receiver would have a step or two coming out of his cut, so he stepped and threw. The receiver bumped the safety with his right shoulder and broke to the sideline. Another perfectly timed, perfectly thrown pass. Another dropped ball.

"[He] made a big catch on that last drive when they got a field goal. But other than that, he's had a terrible day today," said the announcer while watching the replay of the fourth drop. "Good pass protection. Quarterback has time. He steps up and throws a perfect pass. [He] just dropped the ball." It couldn't get any worse. Well, actually, no, it could.

The receiver jumped to his feet and headed to the bench as the punt team took the field. He had his game face on, hiding the certain embarrassment and frustration he felt. Fortunately, his team still had the lead. The punt pinned their opponents back to their own 11 with four minutes and nineteen seconds to go. Time for the defense to do their job.

Eight plays later the receiver saw the lead vanish with a 15-yard touchdown pass and an extra point, making the score 27–23. A field goal would be meaningless. They had to score a touchdown or spend the off-season with the nagging thoughts of being knocked out of the playoffs by the same team for four consecutive years. The receiver would have a lot of time to think about how he had let his teammates down.

They returned the kickoff to the 24. One minute and forty-seven seconds, 76 yards, and three time-outs left. He was on the sidelines for the first three plays of the drive as his team quickly moved the ball beyond midfield. Three more completions and the ball was on the opponent's 25, but they had to burn their last time-out with fourteen seconds. The next pass was nearly intercepted as the clock ticked down to nine seconds.

Nine seconds, time for one play, maybe two. As the ball was snapped, the receiver took off, looking for a seam in the zone that he could split. He didn't see the quarterback stumble when a lineman stepped on his foot as he pulled away from center. He hoped, but couldn't know for sure, that the pocket was holding up long enough for him to get downfield. He had a task to perform and had to trust his teammates to do theirs.

At the 14, the receiver found the seam he was looking for and broke to the post. The quarterback had recovered from his stumble. As his receiver reached the 8-yard line, he stepped and threw. The pass was perfect, just like the other five the receiver had mishandled. The receiver jumped, extended his arms, opened his hands, and spread his fingers. Redemption or the final failure of a miserable day?

The ball hit his right hand, and he clutched it to his chest. His foot hit the ground near the goal line as two defensive backs pin-balled him. He hit the ground, curled, and rolled. Touchdown.

Game won. Confidence salvaged. Super Bowl hopes extended.

"He stuck with it, didn't he? Terrell Owens, he was dropping balls.... Not only did he stick with it, Steve Young stuck with him," said John Madden at the conclusion of San Francisco's 30–27 win over Green Bay in the '98 playoffs.

STICKING WITH IT IN THE MARRIAGE GAME

Whether it's for a game, a season, or a career, sticking with it is an essential quality for a player to make it in the NFL. Terrell Owens came through that day because he stuck with it. And Steve Young stuck with him.

Though he might have felt like giving up altogether or just going through the motions, he didn't. He couldn't. There's a certain measure of accountability in doing what you do in a setting as public as a nationally broadcast NFL game. People would have noticed if he wasn't on the field doing what he was supposed to do. He must have questioned the value of what he was doing, but he couldn't quit.

Unfortunately, quitting is an option for many husbands and wives. Sometimes they quit on themselves. Sometimes they quit on their spouses. They may quit by walking off the field and leaving the relationship altogether. Other times they quit by refusing to invest themselves in the growth of their marriages.

Many people get to a point in their lives where everything they thought their lives were about may be up for grabs. They question the value of their work, the quality of their friendships, the difference they're making in the lives of their kids, the significance of their own lives, maybe even the point of life itself. They may feel squeezed by the changing needs of their children behind them and their aging parents ahead of them. They may have regrets about the past, fears about the future, and serious concerns about today. They may begin to feel that time is running out and that if they don't make changes soon, life will pass them by.

Of all the changes contemplated by people at this time in their lives, changing their marital status is among the most common. They may feel bored and complacent or anxious and insecure. They may feel a resigned malaise or a flailing desperation. They may be tired of feeling that whatever they're doing isn't right or isn't enough. They may feel that their partners are responsible for the way they feel and the way their lives have turned out. They may believe that even though their teammates are the ones who need to change, they aren't going to. They may finally accept what was true all along— that they can't produce lasting change in their partners. And if their partners aren't going to change in the relationship, then they'd better change the relationship. Why stick with it any longer? Why keep trying?

The person at midlife asks a lot of questions: Is my marriage worth it? What did we ever see in each other? What happened to the person I thought I married? If I had it to do over again, would I marry the same person? What made me think we could make it? Is a lifetime marriage even reasonable anymore? Wouldn't every- one—me, my spouse, the kids—be better off if we weren't just going through the motions? Can I ever be happy with this person? Don't I deserve to be happy?

We can dwell on these questions. We can ask them over and over until they become innocuous background music. We rarely notice it, at least consciously, but we're always listening to it. This questioning can happen earlier, but it usually takes awhile for the results of our choices to intertwine with each other and play themselves out. From midlife you may be able to look back and see your past as a path you've been on. And you may have gained enough experience and perspective to feel confident that you can look ahead and know where your life is going.

If you think of it as a midlife crisis with divorce as a definite possibility, it can be a destructive process. Divorce has become a common and accepted solution to the pain and disappointment many people experience in marriage. And blaming our spouses for the breakdown of the relationship makes it easier to move on. But many marriages are set up to fail from the beginning.

Several ideas might explain why we choose the mates we do. Maybe we make sober, well-thought-out decisions based on a thorough examination of our partners' character. We thoughtfully look ahead to the challenges we can expect to encounter based on each other's strengths and weaknesses. We examine our mates' demonstrated ability to adapt to change. We evaluate the passion of their pursuit of Christlikeness. Maybe you did it that way. I didn't. And the number of divorces and unhappy marriages suggest that most people aren't that thorough. Something else must be going on.

Some people believe that we choose our spouses based on a desire to fix what was wrong in the families in which we grew up. So we look for mates who allow us to replicate the dynamics of our families. Or maybe we choose mates whose strength means we won't have to grow or whose weaknesses mean we'll always be needed. Perhaps we choose our partners based on what we think is their ability to meet our needs that were unmet in our childhood. Some attribute our mate choices to a survival-of-the-fittest instinct that drives women to choose men based on their ability to provide food and shelter (material lifestyle) and men to choose women based on their reproductive abilities (physical attractiveness and child-nurturing traits). Maybe there's some truth to these ideas.

These subconscious motivations would certainly help explain why so many people eventually become dissatisfied with their marriages. We are trying to get our spouses and our marriages to do what they cannot do.

We find out our partners can't magically heal old wounds. So we feel betrayed. We get tired of being treated like a child or having to parent our spouses. And we grow rebellious or contemptuous. We finally learn we can't change them or they won't change in ways that are in their best interests (and, oh yes, that might also make our lives easier). So we become frustrated and irritated with them. We discover that material lifestyle and physical attractiveness don't satisfy as we'd expected. We grow disillusioned and start a search for more and different.

We conclude that our spouses are unable or unwilling to do

what they were supposed to do. They are failing us. They are dropping the ball. But what we may feel as disappointment in our
spouses is often a window into our own issues. If we treat this time as
a midlife reassessment, it can be a productive and healthy process for
our marriages and our lives. The doubts and rumblings of dissatisfaction in midlife can alert us to legitimate issues that have needed to be
addressed. Whether it's due to the passage of time or a clearer look at
the future, this time can be a catalyst for finally doing the work.

The marriage game, your marriage, is on the line. Time to step
up. Time to stop wondering about the decisions you made. Regardless of the shortcomings you discover in yourself and your spouse,
it's time to take your game to the next level.

When you feel as though you're blowing it in your marriage or
you're not getting anything out of it, it's a great time to ask yourself
what you're in the marriage for. Not the right-sounding, appropriate
answer, but what's really there. It's also a great time to see whether
you view your commitment to marriage as yes/no or how much.

Owens fumbled away his first reception. He got another
chance. He failed again. He got another chance. He failed a third
time. He got a fourth chance. And he failed a fourth time. He was
given a fifth chance. He dropped his fifth pass. Luckily there was
still time for a sixth. He was ineffective and humiliated, but he
didn't quit. He hung with it till he got it right. Terrell Owens and
Steve Young gave us a template for persevering through the challenges of midlife. You don't give up on yourself. And you don't give
up on your teammate. Owens and Young knew what the team's

overarching goal was—to win the game. There was no doubt in their minds. A marriage team should be as clear about their goal. I have suggested that God's primary purpose for marriage is that we become more like Jesus. A husband and wife need to recognize that through marriage they are acquiring the character of Christ. If that's our primary goal, then quitting on the process isn't an option.

Owens knew what his role was. He was supposed to hang on to passes that were thrown to him. He didn't perform very well for fifty-nine minutes and fifty seconds, but at least he knew what he was supposed to do. As husbands, we're told to love our wives as Christ loved the church. Wives are told to respect their husbands. It's what each of us is called to do, and there are no conditions attached.

With every pass thrown his way, Owens had a way of judging how well he was performing his role. And with each dropped pass, he had his answer. As husbands, we'd be smart to ask ourselves each day how well we have loved our wives. Have we made sure our wives are secure in our love? And wives would benefit from reminding themselves that their primary task in marriage is to convey respect to their husbands. Wives, do your husbands know that regardless of their performance on this day you hold them in high regard? Husbands and wives should keep track of how well they do their own jobs, not how well their spouses do.

When marriages start to flounder, it is rarely a matter of only one spouse not doing his or her job. Though one partner may be legitimately responsible for a disproportionate share of the blame, both contribute. Regardless of where the blame lies, both have some-thing to learn, some way to perform their roles better. The wise spouse steps back and asks some tough questions. There is an *I* in *team.*

How am I doing in my battle against my self-centeredness?

What am I contributing to this problem?

What am I not contributing to this problem? Regardless of what my spouse says, what things am I getting blamed for that are really more his or her issues?

Am I getting the input of a wise person who is committed to the success of my marriage and can speak the truth in love to me?

How can I continue my process of becoming more like Jesus while we're going through this?

Regardless of whether he or she has earned it or accepts it, how can I continue to serve my spouse in ways that are loving and respectful?

The honest spouse takes the time to answer these questions. The courageous spouse takes faithful action and grows as a result. The persevering spouse continues the process even without seeing the desired results, ones he or she may be legitimately entitled to. Whether spouses recognize it or not, their character is growing.

The Atlanta Falcons were getting pounded once by the 49ers. The coach at the time, Jerry Glanville, had a little surprise in store for his players at halftime.

"This game is over. I know and you know we aren't going to win and I don't care...," he told his players. It was halftime heresy, but he continued. "I'm not going to look at the first half of this game on film and you won't see it either. As far as I'm concerned, this thing never happened. But I'll tell you this, I'm gonna look at this second half and see who's with me. I'm gonna look to see who's still playing, even though this thing is out of reach. If you lay down on me, you're finished. If you go out and fight your _____ off, we'll be okay. We may lose this, but if you fight, there'll be another day."

Sometimes you fight for your marriage as an act of faith. You hope you'll turn a corner, but you don't know when or how. The payoff may not come when you expect it in marriage. And it may not come suddenly. As a matter of fact, this midlife wrestling could be a process that takes months or even years. But if both the husband and wife see their marriage as an effective tool for transforming their character and stick with it, they can begin to enjoy the relationship rewards of being more like Jesus.

We will grow in our capacity to love. We will experience a new ability to see ourselves and our spouses as we really are. And we can lovingly accept what we see. We'll better understand both giving and receiving grace. We will be more secure in ourselves, confident in our partners, and grateful for and empowered by our marriages.

As a result, the world becomes, not a place where we go to escape from our marriages, but a place where we continue our transformation with increased purpose and energy. With the foundation of our marriages set, the world becomes a place where we continue the adventure of growth as we consider the relationships we want to invest in, the talents and abilities we want to develop, and the directions we want to explore.

A lot of spouses don't stick with it till they get it right. Terrell Owens did. A lot of spouses don't stick with their teammates till they get it right. Steve Young did. As a result, the 49ers advanced to the next round of the playoffs. They didn't make it to the Super Bowl that year, but two years later Owens was still sticking with it when he set an NFL record with a monster twenty-catch day against the Chicago Bears.

The Extra Point

You're in the San Francisco huddle, down by 4 points, ball on the 25, nine seconds to go. Your hands are on your knees, and you are staring through your face mask at the ground. You lean in toward the center of the huddle so you can hear the play over the roar of the crowd.

"Three-All Jet-Go, on one."

Just before the huddle breaks, you lock eyes with Steve Young. He nods at you twice, slightly but firmly. He shoots you a confident little "this is what it's all about" smile. You're still his go-to guy.

"Don't throw it to me," you say loud enough for all your teammates to hear. Shaking your head, slowly, firmly, defiantly, you continue, "Sorry, I'm tired of fouling up. Count me out. Don't expect me to be there."

Your teammates can't believe what they're hearing. The game is on the line, and you want nothing to do with it. "Sorry," you repeat. "Not me. Not now."

———

Is there an area of your life or relationship in which your wife keeps counting on you and you keep dropping the ball, an area in which you're embarrassed, discouraged, and about to give up? Or maybe you already have?

If your marriage until now has been in the first half, how prepared are you for the second half? Do you have a clear understanding of your team's goals and how you directly contribute to achieving them? Do you believe she respects you? Does she feel absolutely secure in your love? Have you shown the willingness to learn and grow and the determination to take appropriate action steps? Have you demonstrated the resourcefulness necessary to adapt to changing circumstances and the perseverance to stay focused on the goal? How confident in each other are you and your wife as you start the second half?

overtime

*There are coaches who spend eighteen hours a day coaching
the perfect game, and they lose because the ball is oval
and they can't control the bounce of the ball.*

—BUD GRANT

What more could he give? He had already done everything
that was asked of him. He had done more than could be
reasonably expected. In fact, he'd done things nobody had done
before. Now the game was on the line. The season was on the line.
It didn't matter whether or not he had anything left; he had to give
more.

For the second straight year, he had led the league in receptions,
something no other AFC tight end had done even once. But he was
no ordinary tight end. The former first-round draft choice was a
match-up nightmare. At six foot five and 250 pounds, he could over-
power smaller defensive backs. Blessed with a wide receiver's hands
and athleticism, he was difficult for linebackers to keep up with.

Defenses were further confounded by the fact that he lined up
all over the field—split out as a wide receiver, trotting from one side

of the formation to the other as a man in motion, and as a traditional tight end, anchoring the line next to the tackle.

His first reception of this divisional playoff game, an 11-yarder, had provided a glimpse of things to come. A trio of defensive backs had brought him down, delivering a message as they did. He would get his catches, but he was going to pay a price. Another three defenders dragged him down after his second reception, the first of eight first downs he made that afternoon.

A defender popped him with a forearm at every opportunity. They gang tackled him every chance they got. They knew they couldn't stop him but figured the constant pounding, as well as the Florida heat and humidity, would grind him down.

The tight end's team had come into the game as the highest scoring unit in the league. They were loaded. Their featured running back had scored nineteen touchdowns, tying a record, and was the conference's second-leading rusher. His running mate had rushed, received, and returned his way to 2,100 all-purpose yards, the most by a rookie since Gale Sayers in 1965. The quarterback had thrown more completions (360) for more yards (4,802) than any other quarterback in the history of the NFL to that point.

In case all that offensive firepower came up short of the goal line, their kicker was a field goal away from leading the conference in scoring. They were an awesome offensive unit.

However, they entered the game as 3-point underdogs. They were on the road against the conference's stingiest defense. Their own defense had some notoriety too. They were the conference's most generous unit, allowing more points than any other. It figured to be a shootout.

The offense of the tight end's team opened the game with a drive for a field goal. The defense held. They returned the punt 56 yards for a touchdown. They recovered a fumble on the ensuing kick and, four plays later, scored again. An interception and a return to the 12-yard line on the following series led to yet another 6 points. The 24–0 first-quarter lead was more a matter of opportunism than sustained excellence. Still, 24–zip is 24–zip. The rout was on.

Coaches will tell you that the sooner you fall behind, the more time you have to catch up. But coaches are paid optimists. The tight end's team surrendered a field goal and a touchdown, making the score 24–10, as their own offense stalled.

With only six seconds remaining in the half, the defense gave up an inconsequential 15-yard completion. It should have sent the teams into the locker rooms separated by 14 points. Except that as the receiver was being tackled, he lateraled the ball to a trailing back, who raced untouched down the sideline for a touchdown, which narrowed the score to 24–17. The rout was off.

The defense gave up another score on their opponent's first possession of the second half. The teams were tied 24–24, back at ground zero, having matched unanswered 24-point outbursts.

On his team's first possession of the second half, the tight end broke a tackle halfway through a 20-yard catch-and-run before a safety chased him down and forced him out of bounds. Two catches later another three defenders gang tackled him after another first down. Nobody touched him after his next reception, a 25-yard touchdown to put his team back ahead in the third quarter. The defense then gave up a 50-yard touchdown pass to tie the game. After an interception, the hosts scored again to take their first lead of the game at 38–31.

As the tight end gathered in his next reception, a quick slant over the middle, the first defender hit him low, taking away his momentum. A linebacker pinballed him back the other way. Another defender smacked him from behind. The fourth defender drilled him helmet to helmet, trying to drive him into the ground short of the first down.

The tight end not only picked up 10 yards, but a face-mask penalty on one of the defenders gave them another 15. It was the kind of play that inspires a team and hammers at the resolve of their opponents. Except it didn't. Three plays later the drive stalled, and they were forced to punt. Great efforts often aren't directly or immediately rewarded. But for great players, a great effort is not a single play or even a game. It is the approach they bring to the game itself. They just keep pounding away.

They got the ball back on their own 18, trailing 31–38 with four minutes and thirty-nine seconds remaining. Seven plays later his 6-yard reception on third-and-five kept the drive alive. It was his eleventh catch of the day, an NFL playoff record, and his sixth first down. Two plays later he found himself in the end zone, futilely lunging for the barely overthrown pass. His rookie teammate, the productive all-purpose back, had circled out of the backfield and gathered in the errant ball at the back of the end zone for a touchdown. With fifty-eight seconds remaining, the extra point was good, tying the score.

The short kickoff was returned to the 40-yard line with only fifty-two seconds remaining. Four plays later the hosts had driven to the 25 and were lining up for an attempt at the winning field goal.

"Get me some penetration, guys," yelled the tight end to his teammates in the huddle, "so I can have a chance to block it." Are you kidding me? What's an All Pro tight end doing on special teams? Whatever he could to give his team a chance to win the game.

A chance to block it? Maybe earlier in the season, before the nicks and dings of sixteen regular-season games and eighty-eight receptions. Maybe earlier in the game, before the heat and humidity cramped his thighs, calves, and back. Maybe earlier in the fourth quarter, before he threw a brutal blind-side block that broke his shoulder pads and nearly his shoulder as well. He had to find whatever he had left and give it.

A chance? Maybe if he got a running start and timed his jump perfectly. Maybe if he was able to vault himself off some teammate's shoulder. Maybe if he extended his six-foot-five frame as much as he could, stretched his right arm as high as it would go, and spread his hand as wide as possible.

A chance? A slim chance, yes, but a chance nonetheless. It wasn't even a chance to win. The best he could do was to keep his team from losing and extend this epic sufferfest. At the snap he ran and jumped. He pushed off a teammate. He extended himself, stretched his arm, and spread his right hand.

It wasn't one of those blocks that thumps into a defender's outstretched arms. The tight end caught it with his pinkie, robbing it of velocity and elevation. As he fell to the ground, his whole body cramping, the field-goal attempt fluttered harmlessly into the end zone.

Overtime, or more appropriately sudden death, turned out to be anything but sudden. The two teams traded missed field goals and punts for nearly fourteen minutes of the additional period. Each had the ball three times and couldn't put an end to the game. The first team to score might be the last man standing. The fourth time they got the ball, the tight end's team found something they didn't know they had. They quickly moved to their opponents' 11. The coach sent his field-goal team into the game.

More than four hours after the game had begun in hot, muggy Miami, Rolf Benirschke nailed his redemptive kick to give the San Diego Chargers a 41–38 overtime win in the game *Sports Illustrated* judged its all-time favorite game in any sport.

How do you measure tight end Kellen Winslow's performance? A playoff record thirteen catches for 166 yards would give you a clue. The thirteen pounds he lost and a body temperature that registered 105 after he was helped off the field would indicate expended effort. His block of the Dolphins' field-goal attempt at the end of regulation that kept his team in the game would help you understand. But how can you quantify the determination to win regardless of the circumstances?

OVERTIME IN THE MARRIAGE GAME

A player thinks he knows how it's going to be. Everyone brings a set of expectations to the game. If you play the game hard for four quarters, if you play the game fair, you'll win more than you lose. Sometimes the ball takes funny bounces, though. Sometimes sixty minutes aren't enough. A winner doesn't just shrug and say, "That's all I was prepared for. Sorry, that's all I can give. I'm outta here."

"What's it going to take from me to win this game?" is how a winner responds.

Mark had time to prep himself for the big game. He'd married Gail at twenty-six. Two years later Gail was pregnant. Unfortunately, she miscarried. Mark grieved the loss, but like many men, after much discussion he was ready to move on emotionally. However, he saw how differently the miscarriage affected Gail. She wasn't ready to move on. A mother-child bond had already been formed. She felt the loss on a much deeper level than he did. He knew it was real, even if he couldn't understand it.

"We'd talked it over and understood each other as much as possible," says Mark. "She was feeling a loss that I could not fill."

Gail became pregnant again. Once more she miscarried. Six months after losing their first baby, they had to go through the same process all over again. Gail felt the loss even more deeply. Mark was again on the outside looking in. He tried to console his wife, but he wasn't able to understand the significance of what she felt. He was learning, though.

One year later their dream came true, and their family grew to three. When Mark had a baby to hold in his arms, he finally began to understand the bond that Gail had felt. He had looked forward to being a father and mourned the loss of their first two babies, but when at last he had one to hold, that bond was suddenly real to him.

A second son was born three years later. The festive spirit of the delivery room turned instantly professional and matter-of-fact at the moment the newborn entered the world. Mark saw that something was wrong with Kyle's legs, but the doctor quickly whisked him away for tests. Mark was then escorted out of the room. To this day they don't understand why they were separated at their time of greatest uncertainty and need for each other. Forty-five minutes later they were brought back together with Kyle and told that he had been born with bilateral clubfeet. Both of his feet were turned in and upward. It wasn't what Gail or Mark had expected.

Kyle came to them as a special-needs child. At four months Gail wondered why Kyle couldn't lift his head. It wasn't until ten months later, when they discovered how special Kyle was, that she had her answer. He was diagnosed with cerebral palsy.

The ball doesn't always bounce the way you expect, and life doesn't always work out the way it's supposed to. The effort you're prepared to give may not be the effort required to win the game.

Mark had been prepping for this for years, although he hadn't known it.

"The underlying thing is trust and commitment," says Mark.

A wife's greatest need is to be secure in the love of her husband. She needs to know that the man she has committed her life to has committed his life to her. A woman needs a go-to teammate in marriage. She needs to know that he will be there for her.

Mark was there for her through the first miscarriage. He was there through the second, as well. He felt as if he was in a fog at times, unable to either understand Gail or truly comfort her. He didn't have all the answers, but he stayed in the game. He was committed. When he said "for better or worse," he meant it.

"When people get married they should not be thinking, *Is this the person I want to go on fun vacations with and have a nice home with and have healthy kids with?*" advises Gail. "They should be asking, 'Is this the guy I want to go through two miscarriages with and go through financial troubles with and have a special-needs child with?'"

A husband loves his wife. It's a commitment to his teammate he must live out every day. In the process he creates a secure relationship. And a wife respects her husband. That love and respect form the bonds that hold a marriage together, giving it the strength to continue to thrive when extraordinary circumstances suddenly become part of ordinary life. It's a formula for a successful marriage. It takes time, but none of it happens without that steadfast commitment to the marriage team and meeting the needs of your teammate.

Whatever it takes? Yeah, whatever it takes. Thirteen catches, a blocked field goal, and what about those two third-quarter tackles? Near the end of the quarter, San Diego faced a third-and-ten from their own 15. At the snap, Winslow jogged off the line, then cut across the middle at the 30. He was gassed. Chargers' quarterback Dan Fouts found another receiver and let it fly. A little too far. Interception at the San Diego 45.

As the defender cut back across the field with the ball, Winslow caught him from behind and tossed him to the ground. Except— stop me if you've heard this before—as the Miami player was going down, he lateraled to a teammate. Fifteen yards later it was—stop me if you've heard this before—Winslow who caught him from behind and rode him to the ground at the Chargers' 15.

"You find something deep inside you and you push on," says Winslow of finding a strength he didn't know he had. You don't know what you have, or don't have, until circumstances show you. And they will show you with unblinking clarity.

The parents of a special-needs child must face the fact that they are going into overtime against that same old foe: self-centeredness. Their greatest relationship efforts will be required when they may feel like they have the least left to give. More of their emotional energy will be invested in their child, leaving less for each other. At the same time, each may feel their own needs more acutely because of the challenges they are facing. It is the kind of relational dynamic that can destroy a marriage.

Mark and Gail had to prepare for the fact that even though their relationship was still the most important one in their house, it would not receive as much attention as Kyle. Mark and Gail would have to be highly intentional about building their marriage.

There's a common belief that God gives special-needs children to special parents. Gail and Mark don't believe it. The parents of a special-needs child don't appear to be any different from the parents of most children. It's the children that make them special parents. God gives special-needs children to normal parents. Special is what the parents become in the process.

"Our passion is helping parents of special-needs kids get to the blessings," says Gail. They are involved in a ministry to help those parents adapt to the realities they weren't expecting.

The blessings?

Mark notices people hurrying through life. He used to live the same way, always rushing around. Not anymore. A special-needs child will help you slow down, and in the process you'll discover what is really important in life.

"Boy, they miss a lot," is how Mark characterizes so many of the people he sees running through their days, on the go, from one activity to another. Special-needs children also will teach you an entirely different perspective on parenting.

"We know how important it is to discipline without breaking their spirit," Mark says. "The only thing they have is their spirit when their bodies aren't cooperating." They've also learned how important it is to love and empower children according to their own uniqueness. With four boys now, they have a lot of uniqueness to figure out.

Mark and Gail are intentional about their parenting. They have to be, but they have also discovered how important it is to get the basic marriage skills right. A special-needs child will present challenges to a couple's decision making, financial management, conflict resolution, and intimacy. A Super Bowl marriage doesn't happen by accident. The parents of special-needs children are particularly aware of that.

"Wherever you needed work in the relationship before, you'd better expedite it, because this whole thing gears up and gets moving pretty good," Mark advises couples. Some studies place the divorce rate near 85 percent in families where there is a special-needs child. The parents may face more significant decisions in a year than most couples face in a lifetime. The cherished myth that marriage concerns somehow will work themselves out over time? That's a luxury a husband and wife can't afford with a special-needs child in the family.

Whatever weaknesses there are will be exposed. If they are not strengthened, those weaknesses will be the points at which the marriage fractures. It's the kind of intentional problem solving that all couples should employ, but many don't.

A special-needs child is just one example of an unexpected challenge a couple may face. It could be argued that all children have special needs; some needs are just more special than others. A couple may unexpectedly face sudden health issues, a financial reversal, an upheaval in their extended families, and on and on. The list of significant and unexpected challenges is limitless. Winning the marriage game may require skills you don't naturally possess and can't easily develop. And they probably won't develop without that whatever -it-takes commitment to your partner, your marriage, and your own pursuit of a Christlike character.

Kellen Winslow was inducted into the NFL Hall of Fame in 1995. When a player comes up big with millions of people watching, he is remembered as a hero. At least 130 sets of parents were moved enough by his effort in that 1982 playoff game to name their children Kellen. It's a moving tribute to a magnificent game.

People don't know what they are capable of until it is asked of them. A player prepares for those sixty-minute Sunday games, but sometimes it takes more. A man prepares for a normal life in his role as husband and father. Sometimes it takes more. A lot more.

The Extra Point

Funny how these things work out sometimes, you think as you watch the coin fall to the grass. Overtime against your division rivals, a team you'd already beaten twice this year—by 9 and then 10 points. Competitive games, but you were in control. Now it's the playoffs. Win or go home. You were ahead by seven late in the game. But the punt coverage team had a breakdown and gave up a touchdown to tie. You didn't want to be here. You shouldn't be here. But here is where you are. Two wins earlier in the season, ahead by seven late in the game—none of it matters. First team to score moves on.

"Heads," the official says.

Oh well, you think, *I hope the defense has something left.*

<hr/>

In the past, in either your life in general or marriage, how well have you handled unexpected circumstances?

If you encountered a sudden, unexpected challenge that resulted in a permanent change, how confident are you that you would continue to grow as a husband?

The Way the Game's Supposed to Be Played

*I didn't see it as a turning point in the game. I saw it as
an opportunity to follow through on a commitment
I'd made to my teammates.*

—Mike Singletary

here was a moment of truth at the 16-yard line, a split-second cost-benefit analysis as the quarterback, scrambling to elude the rush, considered his options. It was third down, the eleventh play of the drive that had started at his own 7. He was still 10 yards from the first down.

He could play it safe and throw the ball away. He could head for the refuge of the sideline. A field goal was virtual certainty from that range. Or he could turn his thirty-seven-year-old body upfield and challenge the converging defenders for the first down. The third quarter was nearly over. A field goal early in the second quarter had given his team a 17–7 lead. Since that time their offensive efforts had yielded a three-and-out, a fumble on the first play of the second half, and another three-and-out.

Meanwhile their opponents, the defending champions and 12-point favorites coming into the game, had evened the score with a masterful seventeen-play, 95-yard drive to end the first half and a field goal on their first possession of the second. They were back in the game and gaining momentum, on the verge of giving the NFC its fourteenth consecutive Super Bowl victory.

Pressure situations were not new to the quarterback.

In his last college game, his team had trailed 19–17 with only fifty-three seconds remaining. They faced a fourth-and-seventeen from their own 13. He threw a 29-yard rope for a first down. He then maneuvered his team into position for a 35-yard field goal with only four seconds left, to give them an apparent 20–19 victory and postseason bowl trip. With the game on the line, he had delivered. He then watched from the sideline as the California kickoff-return team fielded the ensuing squib kick and, five laterals later, scored one of the most bizarre touchdowns in the history of college football to win the game. It's simply referred to as "The Play."

Perhaps that game was a portent, the beginning of a pattern of accomplishment followed by disappointment.

That spring he was the number one draft pick, the first of six quarterbacks taken in the famous Quarterback Draft of '83. He signed a contract that made him the NFL's highest-paid player before he had even taken a snap. He was in the center ring of a training-camp media circus. In his first action as a pro, he led his team on a ten-play, 75-yard drive in which he completed five of six passes.

"He was awesome in preseason," was the assessment of his coach. "He was the best looking rookie I've ever seen. With so much talent in one individual, I expected him to go out and perform miracles."

The miracles would have to wait. He went from awesome to awful. He totaled only seven touchdowns while throwing fourteen interceptions and ended his rookie season with a 54.9 quarterback rating, ranking him seventeenth in a fourteen-team conference.

Only three years after his disastrous rookie season, he'd come a long way—all the way to the conference championship game. But there was still a long way to go—and a short time to get there. With five minutes and forty-three seconds left in the game and trailing 20–13, he came under his center at his own two as thousands of rabid fans screamed and tossed dog biscuits from the stands. Five minutes and fifteen plays later the quarterback took a shotgun snap from the opponent's 5-yard line. He took his five-step drop, wound up, and cranked an absolute rocket into the stomach of his receiver. Tie game. Their field goal on their first overtime possession propelled them to victory and into the Super Bowl.

Pressure? It was the twelfth time in his young career he had led his team to victory after they had entered the fourth quarter tied or behind. Eventually that total would reach forty-seven, tops in NFL history. Once again he had proven he could rise to the challenge.

A stellar regular season. A magnificent drive in the clutch to advance to the Super Bowl. A win would be the perfect ending.

Unfortunately, they got blown out 39–20. Accomplishment and disappointment, never the promise of one without the threat of the other. The rhythms of football life can be cruel.

The following year his team defended their title as AFC West champions. He earned a return to the Pro Bowl and was honored as the NFL's Most Valuable Player. Once again with a trip to the Super Bowl at stake in the conference championship game, he led his team on a fourth-quarter drive to score the winning touchdown, this time with four minutes and one second remaining.

The first time he touched the ball in the Super Bowl, he threw a 56-yard scoring strike. On his team's second possession, his 32-yard completion was the key play in a drive resulting in a field goal and a 10–0 first-quarter lead. They were set to avenge their loss of the previous season. Instead, they were blown out again, 42–10.

He led his team to an AFC-best 11-5 in '89 and was up to his season-saving playoff theatrics. For the third time he rallied his team to a fourth-quarter playoff victory by driving the offense 71 yards in nine plays to score the winning touchdown with two minutes and twenty-seven seconds left. He followed that up with a 385-yard, three-touchdown performance the following week in the conference championship game, earning a third trip to the Super Bowl. This guy was good.

Perhaps he brought out the very best in his counterparts. Or perhaps he was simply an unlucky foil, unfortunate enough to be on the same field as opposing quarterbacks who performed magnificently. He watched the opposing quarterback throw a Super Bowl–record five touchdown passes to lead a 55–10 rout.

"This is going to live with me, I know that," the quarterback said on his way to the team bus. He was right. He had been the losing quarterback in three of the last four Super Bowls. In spite of all his achievements, his name became synonymous with disappointment.

The rhythms of football life.

It would be six years before they found their way into the play-offs again, but what a return they made. They concluded the regular season with a conference-best 13-3. Their Super Bowl journey would begin at home against the winner of one of the wild-card games. They hadn't lost at home all year. They had an extra week off to repair and prepare as the wild card teams pounded on each other. Their eventual first-round opponent was a two-year-old expansion team, only one season removed from its 4-12 start.

The quarterback's team got off to a 12–0 first-half lead. Then the wheels came off. Their opponents, 14-point underdogs coming into the game, scored on six consecutive possessions to pull off a stunning 30–27 upset. Afterward, the quarterback wept. He had played so well in the regular season. The team had played so well. Then it was over, just like that. Another off-season to wonder if he would ever have another shot at the one thing that had eluded him.

He got his shot again the next year. His 12-4 wild-card team rolled through their three playoff opponents to earn another chance at the Lombardi Trophy, the one thing that would validate his career. Without it, people would remember him as much for what he hadn't accomplished as what he had.

The successes, the disappointments, the could-have-beens and the oh-so-closes—all of that was behind him, and so were nearly three quarters of his fourth Super Bowl. He had a decision to make, quickly. Two lateral steps later he made his choice and turned toward the goal line. No sense holding back now. Who knew if he'd ever have another chance. At the 7, with the strong safety closing from his right and a linebacker and defensive back coming from his left, he leaped for the first down. The first hit helicoptered him 180 degrees; the second drove him into the ground. First-and-goal from the 4.

"When I saw him do that and then get up pumping his fist, I said 'It's on.' That's when I was sure we were going to win," said one of his teammates. And again the quarterback rose to the occasion.

Two plays later his team regained the upper hand on a 1-yard touchdown run to take a 24–17 lead. Their opponents would score again to tie the game, but the quarterback drove his team for a winning fourth-quarter score for the forty-fifth time in his career.

As the game ended, he leaped again, this time into the arms of a teammate. He hugged and was hugged. He thrust his fists into the air and screamed triumphantly. He stabbed an index finger into the night sky. Riding the shoulders of jubilant teammates, he pumped his fist high above the crowd.

At thirty-seven years old, ancient for a starting NFL starting signal caller, Denver's John Elway could finally go out on top. He did go out on top, but after one more season. And one more NFL championship. And one more award, this time as Super Bowl MVP, to conclude his remarkable career.

THE GAME OF HIS MARRIED LIFE

Bumps along the road? Yeah, he'd had a few, but he saved his best for last. If you passed him on the street today, you probably wouldn't stop him for an autograph. Greg's a little heavier and a lot grayer than when he went both ways as a center/linebacker for the Bradley Braves in 1961. He may have lost his physical edge, but his heart is stronger than when he was a young man, stronger than men many years his junior who still play the game.

"When you've got two people trying to outserve each other, then you've got something," Greg once said. He and his wife, Marty, were trying to challenge the thinking of the couples attending a premarital seminar. It's the kind of love that Paul was referring to in Philippians 2. It's the kind of love everyone talks about in premarital seminars and agrees is important. Not everyone is willing to live it, however. He was trying to get these premarrieds used to the idea of focusing on their spouses instead of themselves. He was planting the seeds of servanthood. He was hoping it would become a lifestyle for these couples, not a trite cliché.

"The person is always more important than the issue." It was a seed that had been planted in Greg and Marty's life many years before at a marriage retreat. It became a rallying cry in their marriage, often seeing them through trials and conflicts. They had been together since the homecoming dance their freshman year in high school. They started their marriage team when they were both twenty-one. At twenty-two, they became teammates in parenting. They became a Christian team in their early forties. In their mid-forties, they acknowledged their mutual interest in helping others have stronger marriages and became a marriage mentoring team. There were many shared interests that held their team together.

As a team they raised five children, one of whom nearly died of viral pneumonia at two weeks old. Another endured three reconstructive surgeries. Of course, they faced all the normal challenges of raising kids. They kept a business going through some lean years and helped start a couple of ministries.

Those things don't happen by accident. Neither does a successful marriage team. Over the years Greg and Marty developed some pretty strong habits. When they encouraged that group of earnest premarrieds to serve one another, they were speaking from experience.

At fifty-one, Greg and Marty sat, as a team, in the office of a motion specialist. They were there to find out why the carpal tunnel surgery Marty had undergone had failed to improve her deteriorating handwriting, why she could no longer play the piano, why she felt as though she wasn't communicating well, why she felt as if she "was constantly operating in molasses."

"Yeah, you have Parkinson's," was the doctor's blunt assessment after watching Marty's movements for ten minutes. Marty was relieved, almost joyful. To her it was an explanation for the overwhelming sense she'd had the last couple of years that something wasn't right. Greg was reeling, however. All he knew about Parkinson's was that it had caused his grandmother to shake uncontrollably.

Months later Greg was on a retreat at a California hotel where he and Marty had once stayed. As he stood at the bottom of a stairway looking out over the ocean, he remembered how they had run down those same stairs together and then outside to the beach. They had kicked their shoes off, rolled up their pant legs, and run through the water. It was the stuff of elaborately staged commercials, except there were no camera crews. It was just two people enjoying life, still very much in love after more than thirty-five years together.

Greg was hit hard by how much their life had changed. Run down the stairs? Splash through the water? Marty had difficulty even walking. In the midst of feeling sorry for himself and sad about their future, Greg was struck by another memory from years before.

Now more than ever, the person is more important than the issue, he thought.

The issue had changed; the person hadn't. This issue was not one of those daily housekeeping, task-sharing, or conflict-causing concerns that all couples face. It was Parkinson's, and it was life changing. The habits of serving that Greg had developed over the years with Marty would now be put to the test. He had an important role to play. At a point in life when they should have been enjoying the fruits of lives well lived, they came face to face with their biggest challenge.

"It was tough sometimes," Greg admitted. "There were some things we couldn't do any longer. But we learned to love other things. It was never about the *things*. It was about the two of us, the way we got along, the way we related to each other. We could find other things."

And they did. They could no longer go on walks together, so they went on drives instead. If they went too far to comfortably return home, they would simply find a bed-and-breakfast and spend the night. Marty was never much interested in golf, but she often accompanied Greg in the cart so they could spend time together. Greg, never much interested in antiques, started wandering through little shops with her. It was something they could do together.

They never stopped talking. Even with the Parkinson's as a constant distraction, they still had their date nights during which they would ask each other, "How's our marriage doing? What can we do to make it better?"

"I will never, ever catch up. I'll never catch up in the serving department" was Greg's immediate response when Marty voiced her concern that she was a burden. He meant it. She had been steadfast in her encouragement and support of Greg over the years. It never occurred to him to do otherwise when it was Marty who required a disproportionate amount of care.

A Super Bowl husband develops the habits before he needs them.

Who wouldn't be there for his teammate in her time of greatest need? Greg's response was not "Why me?" or "I'm too old for this" but "How can I serve?" Parkinson's is a tough opponent, one that might have beaten Greg had it not been for the skills and habits of servanthood he had developed.

John Elway's skills were as remarkable as his accomplishments. By any measure, he was one of the NFL's all-time greats. But it wasn't until he left the Super Bowl field a victor that people saw him as a winner. He saved his best for last. He rose to the challenge.

Marty's heart simply stopped beating one morning while Greg was at work. She died without pain while affixing tags to Christmas presents for their grandchildren. She was fifty-nine.

The biggest game of Greg's married life was his last. He went out on top too, serving Marty until she was no longer there to serve. He still misses her and the friendship they shared, but he has no regrets. When his marriage game ended, he could look up at the scoreboard and see that he had come out on top. Was he a perfect husband? No. But through it all he had become so much more like Jesus than he ever would have otherwise. He had won the marriage game.

the extra point

You're out of gas. It's early in the fourth quarter. If the team can just hang on for another fourteen minutes, you're in the Super Bowl. Your opponents have been hammering the ball all day. You're on the bench, elbows on your thigh pads, staring at the ground and suck-ing oxygen. You're wondering how much you have left. Forty-five minutes of 300-pound linemen and 240-pound running backs will do that to you. You're hoping your offense gets something going and takes some time off the clock.

You start thinking about the off-season workouts you blew off. You're thinking about the times you coasted. You knew you weren't at your best when the season started. You'd started some bad work habits, and they carried over into season. You'd seen it in some of your teammates, too. They didn't work as hard as they used to.

"Let's go," says one of your defensive mates. "John just threw an interception. We'd better hold 'em. Come on." You grab your hel-met and hope for the best as you trot out.

―――

Are you forming the daily habits of servanthood in your marriage now that will enable you to withstand the life trials ahead?

Right now in your relationship, what are the two most impor-tant habits you're continuing to develop?

NOTES

Chapter 1: A Little Different Approach

page

5   The epigraph to this chapter is drawn from Ray Didinger, ed., *Game Plans for Success: Winning Strategies for Business and Life from 10 Top NFL Head Coaches* (Chicago: Contemporary Books, 1995), 77.

"[It] still amounts to nothing": Bill Walsh, Brian Billick, and James Peterson, *Finding the Winning Edge* (Champaign, IL: Sports Publishing, 1998), 10.

6   *The Bengals' strategy to use short passes:* Walsh, Billick, and Peterson, *Finding the Winning Edge,* 6–7.

8   *"Water, gimme some water":* Joe Montana and Dick Schaap, *Montana* (Atlanta: Turner Publishing, 1995), 13.

"[He] had that uncanny knack": Montana and Schaap, *Montana,* 13.

"Look for Freddie": Michael W. Tuckman and Jeff Schultz, *The San Francisco 49ers: Team of the Decade* (Rocklin, CA: Prima Publishing, 1989), 137.

9   *"The play has always been called":* Montana and Schaap, *Montana,* 14.

14   *"When I think of Bill Walsh":* Brian Billick, *Developing an Offensive Game Plan* (Champaign, IL: Sagamore Publishing, 1997), 10.

Chapter 2: Winning Isn't Everything

page

17   The epigraph to this chapter is drawn from Ray Didinger, ed., *Game Plans for Success: Winning Strategies for Business and Life from 10 Top NFL Head Coaches* (Chicago: Contemporary Books, 1995), 51.

25   *"He was furious":* John Wiebusch, ed., *Lombardi* (Chicago: Triumph Books, 1997), 168.

Chapter 3: The I *in Team*

page

30   The epigraph to this chapter is drawn from Peter King, "About Face," *Sports Illustrated,* December 3, 2001, 42.

"*He had a devastating influence*": Abby Mendelson, *The Pittsburgh Steelers: The Official Team History* (Dallas: Taylor Publishing, 1996), 81–82.

31   "*There was a frustration*": Jack Clary, *The Gamemakers* (Chicago: Follett Publishing, 1976), 143.

33   "*Becoming a winner*": Clary, *The Gamemakers,* 141.

37   *Husbands don't have to earn respect:* Emerson Eggerichs, *Love and Respect: The Respect He Desperately Needs* (Nashville: Integrity Publishers, 2004), 55.

39   "*I firmly believe that*": Mendelson, *The Pittsburgh Steelers,* 118.

40   "*When a husband feels disrespected*": Eggerichs, *Love and Respect,* 18.

41   "*the Energizing Cycle*": Eggerichs, *Love and Respect,* 115.

42   "*I felt sometimes when*": Mendelson, *The Pittsburgh Steelers,* 114.

Chapter 4: The New Guy in the Middle

page

45   The epigraph to this chapter is drawn from "Inside the NFL," *Sports Illustrated,* November 6, 2000, 99.

46   "*Every once in a while*": John Mullin, "Urlacher Is Learning Fast," *Chicago Tribune,* July 26, 2000.

"*This combination of size*": Skip Bayless, "Urlacher Would Revive Bears' Linebacker Legacy," *Chicago Tribune,* April 13, 2000.

"*We thought he'd grow*": Mullin, "Urlacher Is Learning Fast."

"*He still has far too many*": John Mullin, "Injuries, Growing Pains Leave Strength of Bears' Draft Unclear," *Chicago Tribune,* August 16, 2000.

"*I knew it was going to be an adjustment*": Mullin, "Injuries, Growing Pains."

47   *"I just don't have any technique":* John Mullin, "Urlacher Out of Starting Lineup," *Chicago Tribune,* August 23, 2000.

49   *"It definitely wasn't easy":* K. C. Johnson, "Urlacher Flashes Potential as Starter," *Chicago Tribune,* September 18, 2000.

58   *"I think I made more mistakes":* Johnson, "Urlacher Flashes Potential."

Chapter 5: A Fool for a Coach

page

60   The epigraph to this chapter is drawn from George Hetzel Jr., ed., *The Coaches' Little Playbook* (Nashville: Cumberland House, 1996), 83.

61   *"You can go to the bank":* Bob Carroll and others, *Total Football: The Official Encyclopedia of the National Football League,* ed. Matthew Silverman (New York: HarperCollins, 1999), 1790.

   "He's forgotten more football": Michael Silver, "One Tough Customer," *Sports Illustrated,* April 26, 1999, 62.

62   *"The very basis of coaching":* Bill Walsh and Glenn Dickey, *Building a Champion* (New York: St. Martin's Press, 1990), 152.

63   *"[He] has developed":* Silver, "One Tough Customer."

   "I learned more about football": San Francisco 49ers, The Bobb McKittrick Memorial Tribute, 2000.

   "I'd rather teach": Silver, "One Tough Customer."

   officer in the marines: San Francisco 49er 1999 Media Guide.

   "[He] is the spirit": San Francisco 49ers, McKittrick Memorial Tribute.

64   *"I found out a long time ago":* San Francisco 49ers, McKittrick Memorial Tribute.

   "If anybody around here": San Francisco 49ers, McKittrick Memorial Tribute.

   "Check out the Super Bowl": Joe Montana with Richard Weiner, *Joe Montana's Art and Magic of Quarterbacking* (New York: Henry Holt, 1997), 89.

66   *Living together before marriage a hindrance to success:* Glenn T. Stanton, *Why Marriage Matters: Reasons to Believe in Marriage in a Postmodern Society* (Colorado Springs: Piñon Press, 1997), 57–58.

69   *"hook you, grab you":* Tim Green, *The Dark Side of the Game* (New York: Warner Books, 1997), 99.

      "Dr. Mean": Green, *The Dark Side of the Game,* 98.

      "Men who let their wives": John M. Gottman and Nan Silver, *The Seven Principles for Making Marriage Work* (New York: Three Rivers Press, 1999), 100.

70   *"Research shows that a husband":* Gottman and Silver, *The Seven Principles,* 109.

      Women accept influence from their husbands: Gottman and Silver, *The Seven Principles,* 100.

72   *"We either overcompensate":* Harville Hendrix, *Getting the Love You Want: A Guide for Couples* (New York: Henry Holt, 2001), 19.

Chapter 6: Playing Hurt

page

75   The epigraph to this chapter is drawn from Joe Montana with Richard Weiner, *Joe Montana's Art and Magic of Quarterbacking* (New York: Henry Holt, 1997), 83.

      "When [he] didn't get up": Paul Zimmerman, "One-Man Gang," *Sports Illustrated,* January 10, 1994, 34.

76   *"I think we got":* Mike Freeman, *Bloody Sundays: Inside the Dazzling, Rough-and-Tumble World of the NFL* (New York: William Morrow, 2003), 69.

77   *"[He] is a luxury":* Leigh Montville, "A Man of Vision," *Sports Illustrated,* February 14, 1994, 142.

79   *"From that moment on":* Emmitt Smith and Steve Delsohn, *The Emmitt Zone* (New York: Crown Publishers, 1994), 5.

      "Are you okay?": Smith and Delsohn, *The Emmitt Zone,* 6.

"No way I was sitting down": Smith and Delsohn, *The Emmitt Zone,* 6.

"In my mind, this is still": Rudy Klancnik, *Emmitt: Run with History* (Dallas: Calvert Group, 2002), 44.

80 *"Football is not for the weak":* Klancnik, *Emmitt,* 39.

83 *"In a league as violent":* Smith and Delsohn, *The Emmitt Zone,* 4.

84 *Jim Otto's 38 major surgeries:* Jim Otto with Dave Newhouse, *Jim Otto: The Pain of Glory* (Champaign, IL: Sports Publishing, 2000), 3.

85 *"The soldier would use":* Lee Strobel, *The Case for Christ* (Grand Rapids, MI: Zondervan, 1998), 195.

"He would have been laid down": Strobel, *The Case for Christ,* 197.

86 *"The reason is that the stresses":* Strobel, *The Case for Christ,* 198.

Chapter 7: The Will to Prepare

page

91 The epigraph to this chapter is drawn from Mike Shanahan and Adam Schefter, *Think Like a Champion* (New York: HarperCollins, 1999), 97.

94 *"When you see the linebacker":* Mike Singletary with Jerry Jenkins, *Singletary on Singletary* (Nashville: Thomas Nelson, 1991), 53.

95 *"By that time I'd seen that play":* Mike Singletary in discussion with the author, spring 2001.

100 *"enhance your love maps":* John M. Gottman and Nan Silver, *The Seven Principles for Making Marriage Work* (New York: Three Rivers Press, 1999), 47.

102 *"If there's one thing":* Singletary with Jenkins, *Singletary on Singletary,* 4–5.

Chapter 8: The Block That Won the Super Bowl

page

104 The epigraph to this chapter is drawn from George Hetzel Jr., ed., *The Coaches' Little Playbook* (Nashville: Cumberland House, 1996), 106.

105 *"He's back to throw"*: Quarterbacks on Quarterbacks: The NFL's Top 15 Quarterbacks in Action, videocassette (New York: NFL Films, Inc., 1995).

111 *postpartum depression:* Mayo Clinic staff, "Postpartum Depression," Mayo Clinic, www.mayoclinic.com.

113 *"When Steve Young made"*: Bill Walsh and Glenn Dickey, *Building a Champion* (New York: St. Martin's Press, 1990), 248.

Chapter 9: When It Mattered Most

page

117 The epigraph to this chapter is drawn from Abby Mendelson, *The Pittsburgh Steelers: The Official Team History* (Dallas: Taylor Publishing, 1996), 121.

"Somewhere between now": Broadcast of NFC Championship Game, January 23, 2000, on FOX.

"What if I were to run": Kurt Warner with Michael Silver, *All Things Possible* (New York: HarperCollins, 2000), 217.

119 *"The greatest single-season sports story"*: Warner with Silver, *All Things Possible,* 173.

120 *"Let's go for it"*: Warner with Silver, *All Things Possible,* 217.

121 *"That's a play"*: Broadcast of NFC Championship Game, January 23, 2000, on FOX.

122 *"Contrary to popular belief"*: Howard Markman, Scott Stanley, and Susan L. Blumberg, *Fighting for Your Marriage* (San Francisco: Jossey-Bass, 1994), 1.

69 percent of conflicts are perpetual: John M. Gottman and Nan Silver, *The Seven Principles for Making Marriage Work* (New York: Three Rivers Press, 1999), 130.

126 *Four negative patterns of handling conflict:* Markman, Stanley, and Blumberg, *Fighting for Your Marriage,* 13–34.

128 *"Whenever there was any pressure"*: Warner with Silver, *All Things Possible,* 35.

"I can't overstate how much": Warner with Silver, *All Things Possible,* 35.

130 *Levenson and Carter research on stress:* Gottman and Silver, *The Seven Principles,* 37.

Gender responses to conflict: Gottman and Silver, *The Seven Principles,* 38.

Chapter 10: The Only Thing That's Constant

page

133 The epigraph to this chapter is drawn from Ray Didinger, ed., *Game Plans for Success: Winning Strategies for Business and Life from 10 Top NFL Head Coaches* (Chicago: Contemporary Books, 1995), 20.

"You need to get me": Thomas Boswell, Shirley Povich, and David Sell, et al., *Redskins: A History of Washington's Team* (Washington, DC: Washington Post Books, 1997), 123.

134 *"I'm bored. I'm broke":* Tom Callahan, "Sad Season, Glad Super Bowl," *Time,* February 14, 1983, 64.

"Load up the wagon": Boswell, Povich, and Sell, *Redskins,* 145–46.

135 *"The truly great people":* Paul Zimmerman, "Hail to the Redskins," *Sports Illustrated,* February 7, 1983, 16.

136 *"I don't have to play":* Paul Zimmerman, "One Super Show," *Sports Illustrated,* February 8, 1988, 14.

139 *"Transition is the way":* William Bridges, *The Way of Transition: Embracing Life's Most Difficult Moments* (Cambridge: Perseus Books, 2001), 3.

Chapter 11: The Drive

page

148 The epigraph to this chapter is drawn from Troy Aikman, *Aikman: Mind, Body and Soul* (Chicago: Benchmark Press, 1998), 35.

"We never stop working": Joe Montana, *Joe Montana's Art and Magic of Quarterbacking* (New York: Henry Holt, 1997), 27.

149 *"Get the ball to somebody":* Montana, *Art and Magic,* 177.

152 *"probably the best pass":* Montana, *Art and Magic,* 181.

153 *"Actually this drive is still":* Montana, *Art and Magic,* 181.

Five love languages: Gary Chapman, *The Five Love Languages: How to Express Heartfelt Commitment to Your Mate* (Chicago: Northfield Publishing, 1995), 39, 55, 73, 87, 103.

156 *"two of the most crucial elements":* John M. Gottman and Nan Silver, *The Seven Principles for Making Marriage Work* (New York: Three Rivers Press, 1999), 61–76, 63.

157 *"If you've ever gotten stuck":* Joe Montana and Dick Schaap, *Montana* (Atlanta: Turner Publishing, 1995), 100.

159 *"'The Drive' was the culmination":* Bill Walsh, Brian Billick, and James Peterson, *Finding the Winning Edge* (Champaign, IL: Sports Publishing, 1998), 282.

Chapter 12: Outside the Box

page

163 The epigraph to this chapter is drawn from Glen Liebman, ed., *Football Shorts: 1,001 of the Game's Funniest One-Liners* (Chicago: Contemporary Books, 1997), 83.

"A wonderful clutch performer": Bill Walsh and Glenn Dickey, *Building a Champion* (New York: St. Martin's Press, 1990), 30.

167 *"You bet I batted it":* Will McDonough, Peter King, and Paul Zimmerman, *75 Seasons: The Complete Story of the National Football League, 1920–1995* (Atlanta: Turner Publishing, 1994), 239.

Chapter 13: Coming Back

page

177 The epigraph to this chapter is drawn from Joe Montana with Richard Weiner, *Joe Montana's Art and Magic of Quarterbacking* (New York: Henry Holt, 1997), 174.

179 *"Whatever happens, you guys":* Peter King, "Wild Wild Card," *Sports Illustrated,* January 11, 1993, 38.

One play at a time: King, "Wild Wild Card."

184   *"One of the worst consequences":* Dr. Patrick Carnes, *Out of the Shadows: Understanding Sexual Addiction* (Center City, MN: Hazelden Publishing and Educational Services, 2001), 24.

185   *"Triple A Engine":* Al Cooper, *Cybersex: The Dark Side of the Force* (New York: Brunner-Routledge, 2000), 6.

186   *"The addict substitutes":* Carnes, *Out of the Shadows,* 14.

Chapter 14: Keeping Your Head in the Game

page

193   The epigraph to this chapter is drawn from Phil Barber and John Fawaz, *NFL's Greatest: Pro Football's Best Players, Teams, and Games* (New York: Dorling Kindersley, 2000), 15.

195   *"I don't think I've ever seen":* John Madden, the broadcast of the NFC Wild Card Game, January 3, 1999, on FOX.

197   *"[He] made a big catch":* Madden, broadcast of the NFC Wild Card Game.

199   *"He stuck with it, didn't he?":* Madden, broadcast of the NFC Wild Card Game.

205   *"This game is over":* Tim Green, *The Dark Side of the Game* (New York: Warner Books, 1997), 207.

Chapter 15: Overtime

page

209   The epigraph to this chapter is drawn from Ben Carroll and Michael Gershman, *Total Football II: The Official Encyclopedia of the National Football League* (New York: HarperCollins, 1999), 1789.

213   *"Get me some penetration":* Rick Reilly, "A Matter of Life and Sudden Death," *Sports Illustrated,* October 25, 1999, 136.

214   Sports Illustrated's *all-time favorite game:* Richard Hoffer, "Our Favorite Games," *Sports Illustrated,* October 25, 1999, 122.

218   *"You find something deep inside":* Reilly, "A Matter of Life," 140.

220   *Divorce rate in families with special-needs children:* Cheri Fuller and Louise Tucker Jones, *Extraordinary Kids* (Nashville: Word, 1998), 167.

221   *Children named Kellen:* Reilly, "A Matter of Life," 143.

Chapter 16: The Way the Game's Supposed to Be Played

page

223   The epigraph to this chapter is drawn from Mike Singletary in discussion with the author, spring 2001.

225   *"He was awesome in preseason":* James Beckett, *John Elway* (Dallas: Beckett Publications, 1999), 48.

227   *"This is going to live with me":* Paul Zimmerman, "The Storm," *Sports Illustrated,* February 5, 1990, 20.

228   *"When I saw him do that":* Michael Silver and others, "Seven Up," *Sports Illustrated,* February 2, 1998, 50.